WITHDRAWN

Historical Papers of the
Trinity College Historical Society
Series XXIX

THE LITERARY CAREER
OF
NATHANIEL TUCKER

1750-1807

BY

LEWIS LEARY

DURHAM, NORTH CAROLINA
DUKE UNIVERSITY PRESS
1951

PRINTED IN THE UNITED STATES OF AMERICA BY
THE SEEMAN PRINTERY, INC., DURHAM, N. C.

For
Carolyn

INTRODUCTION

This attempt to reconstruct the trials and achievements of a very minor eighteenth-century man of literary ambition is based almost entirely on letters which he wrote when enthusiasm rose high within him. If then the resulting portrait is distorted to the exclusion of mundane, day-by-day activities or any real sense of the young poet's relationship to the world about him, it is because Nathaniel Tucker was himself less articulate in detailing these. Whenever possible, I have allowed him to speak for himself, in his own words, to present the temper of his own personality without distortion. When he does not speak or when his words need simple explanation, then only have I attempted to speak for him or to supply the backgrounds necessary to an understanding of what he said. The canvas is not large, nor is the composition, I hope, confused with unnecessary detail: our attention will be focused on a well-meaning literary aspirant who stood at the center of his world.

For almost twenty years Nathaniel Tucker worked in poetry, both because of the distinction promised by literary success and because of the opportunity which literature seemed to offer him, to guide and to inspire. In idea and expression he was imitative, a weathercock almost, turning successively to each of the gusty influences which disturbed the end of his century. He composed first, in the 1770's, on the pattern of Goldsmith and Gray, in regularized couplets, in the spirit of humane rationalism derived from Pope. In the 1780's he discovered the free, sweeping lines of Milton and Shakespeare better fitted to the expanding ideology of that revolutionary decade. By the 1790's he had become fascinated by the transcendental revelations of Emanuel Swedenborg and translated them into English which was read by William Blake, Samuel Taylor Coleridge, and many another forward-looking young man at that time. Thus, just because he was a very minor poet, without great originality, Nathaniel Tucker and his reachings for expression may serve the historian as an individual instance of what in larger measure was happening to literature in English as it moved toward the nineteenth century.

Beyond this, however, his story seems worth telling on two counts. Here is a record, remarkably detailed, of the strivings and the failure of a young man who sincerely and with most fervent intensity wanted to be a poet, to express the half-formed notions which swirled excitingly through his head. He probably knew and thought less about the origin of these notions than we shall, as we recognize in his writings phrases culled from books he must have read, catchwords known to be the stock in trade of every literary jack of his time, and ideas the property of most thinking men of his and preceding generations. He never found an idiom of his own, and he never wrote a completely successful poem, but in his efforts and his shortcomings we may, if we will, read a parable pertinent to other men of aspiration in his or in any other time.

Finally, the literary adventures of Nathaniel Tucker are here recorded simply as a poignantly human story, never before completely told, which has been preserved to us by the happy circumstance that the poet's younger brother seems never to have thrown away a letter and that his descendants for many generations have carefully preserved his horde. We shall misread the story, I think, if we find Nathaniel Tucker conspicuously different from or superior to many other talented young men of his time, who were not so fortunate as he in having careful brothers, but who trod, like him, the road of best intentions with high-hearted good will.

The principal materials from which this biographical essay is constructed are letters from or about Nathaniel Tucker in the Tucker-Coleman Collection at Colonial Williamsburg. Most of the correspondence concerned with events discussed in the first four chapters has appeared serially in the *Bermuda Historical Quarterly* since February, 1946. A comparison of my transcriptions with the more exact copies there printed will indicate that I have taken some liberties by writing out Nathaniel's numerous abbreviations (such things as "wou'd" or "woud," "opp'r," and "doct'"), by disregarding his excessive capitalization (except where it is clearly intended for emphasis), by modernizing his spelling so that it will not seem merely quaint, and by substituting periods for the hurried dashes with which he often separated sentences. In all other matters I have attempted as exact a copy and as scrupulous a selection as possible.

In preparation of this essay I am indebted most deeply to the late George P. Coleman and to Mrs. Coleman for their gracious assistance and encouragement, both in supplying materials and in allowing me to talk at length with them about the oldest literary Tucker. Grants in aid from the Research Council of Duke University and from the Institute of Early American History and Culture have made possible the investigations necessary to round out details of Nathaniel Tucker's career. Douglass and Virginia Adair, Carl Bridenbaugh, Lewis Patton, Clarence Gohdes, Lester J. Cappon, and Paull Franklin Baum have each read the story of Nathaniel Tucker in manuscript; if I had been able to take advantage of all their suggestions, it would now be better told. The library staffs at Colonial Williamsburg, at the College of William and Mary, and at Duke University have been unsparing in assistance. Dorothy Roberts has been patient through many drafts in helping me prepare the manuscript, and Carolyn has been impatient that so small a thing should have taken so long.

L. L.

Duke University.

CONTENTS

THE LITERARY CAREER
OF
NATHANIEL TUCKER

1750–1807

I

BERMUDA

The great plenty of fish, which constitutes the chief food of the
people of the island . . . renders them very prolific. The great
salubrity of the air may also have some share in this quality, which
is so remarkable here, that it is no uncommon thing to see 14 or
15 children in every house you come to. . . . Had these people
the means of education, in proportion to their genius and abilities,
they would certainly produce men whose attainments would be an
honour to human nature.

PHILIP FRENEAU, "Account of the Island of Bermuda," 1776

MEMBERS OF the Tucker family have lived in Bermuda almost from
the beginning of its colonial history. Captain Daniel Tucker, one
of the gentlemen adventurers at Jamestown mentioned in John
Smith's *History of Virginia*, served on the island as its second governor from 1616 until his death ten years later. George Tucker
of Gravesend, near Milton, heir to extensive properties in County
Kent—perhaps a nephew of the doughty Captain Daniel—settled in
Bermuda during the Civil Wars of the early seventeenth century,
and his son, also George, died there in 1662. The latter's oldest
son, St. George—the first of many in his family to bear that now
distinguished name and the first Tucker who we can be sure was
born on the island—fathered six sons and, as old records laconically
add, "several daughters." His oldest son, Henry, lived almost sixty
years in Bermuda, where he became a member of the island Council and had four sons, three of whom were lost at sea in voyages
through the treacherous, gale-swept waters of the Caribbean. But
Henry's second son, and his namesake, survived several years of
service in the British army to live to the age of seventy-four and
to bring up during the middle of the eighteenth century his own
four sons and two daughters at the family estate in Southampton
Parish, near Port Royal on the western shore.

Relationships among the Tuckers are at best confusing. Theirs
is a family pride in family names which are handed down, from
father to son, from uncle to nephew, often duplicated—and sometimes more than once—in the same generation. So it was when
Colonel Henry Tucker's oldest child, his daughter Frances, married
her distant cousin, Henry Tucker of the "Bridge House" at Somer-
set; and then, four years later, his oldest son, also named Henry,

married another Frances, the daughter of Governor George James Bruère. This last event took place in 1770, when the Colonel's oldest son was twenty-eight, his youngest eighteen, and the family for one practical reason or another was breaking up. For several years the Tucker children had been leaving home, until now only the twenty-three-year-old spinster Elizabeth, known to her brothers as Sister Bet, remained at "The Groves" near Port Royal. Young Henry had moved with his bride to the other end of the island, to St. George, the seat of colonial government, where, under the patronage of his father-in-law, he was appointed treasurer to the Council and began the political career which was to find him, successively, a member of the Council, its President, and, for a short period later in life, acting Governor of Bermuda.

Even the younger persons were gone. Thomas Tudor had been away for several years in Edinburgh, and now at twenty-six he received his medical degree with the publication of a tightly written dissertation in Latin on—of all things for a native of sunny Bermuda—the effect of cold on the human body. Twenty-year-old Nathaniel had been for two years a clerk to the Council at the island capital, waiting an opportunity to follow his brother in the study of medicine abroad. St. George at eighteen lived with an aunt and uncle named Slater at Belle-Vue, not far from St. George, where he was being tutored by the Reverend Alexander Richardson in preparation for entrance to one of the Inns of the Temple in London. Our immediate interest lies in these three, the younger sons of Colonel Henry Tucker, and particularly in Nathaniel— "poor Natty," they soon were to call him—who became a poet and who was never as successful in worldly affairs as any of his brothers.

All the family were agreed that the retrospective description of home life at Port Royal which Nathaniel wrote two years later was not only greatly poetical, but true—"a faithful picture," his younger brother acknowledged it, "of a family in which I venture to affirm there was never a moment's interruption of the most perfect harmony, parental tenderness, filial piety and affection." Nathaniel described the spreading lawns which descended from "The Groves," lined with cypress trees, and with a little hill on either side covered with low-growing shrubs of evergreen. He remembered the rose gardens, the heavy-scented guava, the woodbine, nasturtium, lilac, and jasmine. The sandy stretch of beach below the house and the wave-splashed promontories which cut into the sea beyond it, the cool shade of olive groves, the unhurried ease, the pastoral simplicity of life amid the sloping hills and emerald-tinted inlets of Bermuda were woven by him into an idyll of his island home:

> Hail Nature's Darling Spot! enchanted Isle!
> Where vernal Blooms in sweet Succession smile!
> Where, cherish'd by the fostering Sea-born Gale,
> Appears the tall Palmetto of the Vale;
> The rich Banana, Tenant of the Shade,
> With Leaf broad spreading to the Breeze display'd;
> . . . .
> The fragrant Lime, the Lemon at his Side,
> And golden Orange, fair Hesperia's Pride;
> While genial Summer, who, approaching fast,
> Claims to disperse the short-liv'd wintery Blast,
> O'er the green Hill and Cedar-bearing Plain
> Boasts, undisturb'd, a long protracted Reign.

Even later he remembered in vivid detail the "bloody conflict" between islanders and a whale, a "huge Leviathan," which had strayed "from his pastures of the deep" to lie landlocked in one of the Bermuda coves, "bellowing enormous," while his tormenters

> with strenuous lance,
> Barbed harpoon and darts of missile death
> Urg'd on the fierce onset, cruelly beset
> Not vanquish'd, but with loss of all their arms
> Themselves were foil'd; for floundering at the pain
> Of deep inflicted wounds, the grand Sea-monster
> Now here, now there, essays his passage back
> To the unfathom'd main, and bounds and plunges
> Lashing the hoary surge with his huge tail
> Boisterous and loud, till now at last the channel
> Between you and the promontories he explores
> Sailing victorious from the blood-stain'd shore
> Amidst their shouts, who on the peopled sea
> In winged skiffs, beheld him like an island
> Floating, his dusky rind transfixt with spears
> A forest rear'd above the watry plain.

As he grew older, he recalled legends of Bermuda—how in times long past "a shoal of witches" journeyed there "from the bay of the Massachusetts" to despoil the enchanted island of its treasures and carry them off to the colder climes of Europe. It was an allegory perhaps, meant to apply to Bermuda's difficult role as a non-combatant during the Revolution, for rosemary, the symbol of fidelity, was the principal object of the raid made by these "with-

ered habitants of air," who came, not on broomsticks, but in a
ship which they packed tight with stolen cargo, while loyal native
fishermen, weary with toil, watched helpless.

But though Bermuda was in retrospect a garden spot filled with
all tropical joys and adventures and legends, it was not always completely satisfactory in supplying the more practical requisites of a
full life. It was quiet and idyllic, but in many respects it was inert,
and becoming more so. If one had money enough, he might live
there very happily indeed, thought Philip Freneau when he visited
the island a few years later; but there were few opportunities for
a young man with his way to make in the world. He might fish
or gorge on a diet of fish to the benefit of his posterity, but markets
for so common a commodity were limited. There was little land
for extensive cultivation, hardly enough for family truck gardens,
and they were cared for by Negroes, who made up fully half the
island population. He might make boats or supervise the making
of boats by slaves adept in handicraft, or he might dare the seas,
as did so many Bermudians, in the carrying trade. Recently, however, restrictive regulations by the Parliament of England had made
such commerce less profitable than it had been, so that now, as
Colonel Tucker observed, the crews benefited more greatly than
the owners. To be sure, an active young man might patrol the
shoals and reefs watching for wrecks, occasionally profitable as sal-
vage. He might even entice unwary ships ashore by false lights,
as it was sometimes whispered the less scrupulous managed to do.

None of these occupations, however, was quite suitable for the
sons of aristocratic Colonel Tucker, who "loved the animated life
of London" and who resided there for extended periods as agent
for Bermuda. They had been trained, as far as facilities on the
island permitted, for more dignified professions, for law, medicine,
and government, professions in which a gentleman might prosper.
In order to complete such training, residence at a university in the
British homeland was essential. Yet during these years just preceding the American Revolution the Colonel, like many other
colonials, felt the pinch of poverty. Goods were scarce, even food-
stuffs, and money was scarcer. Many islanders were leaving for the
mainland, for South Carolina or Virginia, where perhaps they
might prosper with fewer hardships. By 1770 it was clear to him
that his project of sending his two younger sons abroad for study
was, at least for the present, out of the question.

Everyone was disappointed. Thomas Tudor had been writing

with some condescension, but nonetheless glowingly, of his course of study and his student pleasures in Edinburgh. When the younger boys countered by telling him proudly of grand theatrical performances now presented on the island, probably by the American Company under David Douglass, he replied with good-natured sarcasm which could only have made his brothers wish more than ever that they shared his British-bred collegiate sophistication:

I am glad to hear you are become so polished a people as to have a theatre established among you. Assemblies you have had for a long time. What will be next introduced? I think you cannot do without an oratorio. How shall I know little Bermuda after such wonderful improvements? I could not help smiling when I saw the mention of players, for I must confess they are an importation I little expected to hear of. It is somewhat of a droll idea that I have of your theatre. Very magnificent, no doubt! However, I am very glad when I hear you have any new source of entertainment, and things of this kind, however short of perfection, are amusing both by their own novelty and by affording topics of conversation.

The Tuckers never seemed to run out of conversation. Mrs. Tucker interspersed her letters to the boys at St. George with such small domestic intelligence as the fate of their brood of guinea hens or the apparent failure of their experiment in pineapple culture. She attempted to soften their disappointment by affectionate explanation: "I wish Papa's affairs would permit him to send you to school in England immediately but fear he is too much straitened for money just at this time to do it: in a year or two he may perhaps have it in his power to settle matters in a way to make it easy for him." She assured her sons that "nothing but utter incapacity" prevented their "best of fathers" from satisfying their every wish: "Fortune seems to take pleasure in disappointing the plans he makes for fixing them genteely in life." At the same time Sister Bet helped lighten the blow by chatting to her brothers of local gossip, who had married whom, and who was disappointed, who expected babies, and how soon. Their father wrote more straightforwardly, as befitted a man communicating with grown sons. He regretted his inability to provide for them as he had planned. Meanwhile, he advised them of the pitfalls besetting young men away from home: "Above all things be cautious of your company. Youth are too apt to be drawn away by folly. . . . Let all your actions be dictated by honor and virtue, and then you are sure of living right."

Such admonition may have been taken to heart by the two boys at St. George, though there could have been little comfort in it. Thomas Tudor, now Dr. Tucker and ready to set up in practice, stopped off at home to complete plans for settling at Charleston in South Carolina, where so many Bermudians had recently emigrated, and where he might be expected to find better medical opportunities than in his impoverished native island. Friends in Virginia had written the Colonel with enthusiasm of the College of William and Mary in Williamsburg, not only of the excellence of its training, particularly in law, but also of its inexpensiveness. St. George would study there, at least until times were better.

And Nathaniel? There seemed little for him to do in Bermuda. His clerkship must have occupied only a portion of his time, and, for all its occasional theater and its official balls, St. George was not an exciting place for a young man. Nathaniel wrote to his sister:

> In this poor Town there's nothing done
> There's neither Merriment nor Fun,
> There's nothing clever, nothing new,
> The same dull Scene recurs to View.

At least, he might get away from it, might follow his physician brother to South Carolina and work with Thomas Tudor there as an apprentice and assistant, while they earned enough money to pay for his education. By this means he could with industry better prepare himself for his medical course in Edinburgh—if he ever did get there.

The Tuckers were a close-knit and affectionate family, who enjoyed writing long letters to one another, detailing each daily activity. Better than that, from our point of view, they guarded family letters with care, so that today packages of old correspondence yield not only the outlines of the activities of the three Tucker boys who came to America in 1771, but also the ups and downs of their mercurial dispositions as they faced one after another the inevitable disappointments and discouragements of growing into manhood.

Most articulate of them all was Nathaniel, already known and appreciated by the family for talent with his pen. They enjoyed him as a poet, were proud of his clever, light-hearted verses, but seemed at this stage to take him only half seriously, for—whatever his promise—he seldom was pretentious and wrote only simple, polite little poems, such as St. George liked to write also, and at which even Sister Bet and Brother Tommy were not averse to trying their less practiced hands. Nathaniel composed acrostics or gentle compliments "To Belinda in the Country" or "To Miranda," the kind of verse that any sprightly young man might write to make himself socially, even flirtatiously, more acceptable.

The Tuckers were a cultured family, who knew good poetry and respected and admired it. There are legends of cool, shaded afternoons among the olive groves above the house when Nathaniel read to his sisters from their favorites, from Goldsmith and Gray and Pope. But it was apparently not until after he had left Bermuda and, with proper eighteenth-century romantic sensibility, felt nostalgic pangs at being what he called exiled from his happy native isle, that Nathaniel really attempted serious verse. Meanwhile, now from St. George, he entertained his sisters with facetious doggerel, reminiscent of the good times which they and their brother "Saint" had formerly enjoyed at "The Groves":

> Methinks I'm now among you all
> Parading it about the Hall—
> St. George appears with Bus'ness fraught—
> Th' electrical Machine is brought—
> He screws it down upon the Table
> And runs it hard as he is able—
> At length prepar'd, I see you stand
> Around the Table Hand in Hand—
> The Wire touch'd, you feel the Shock—
> One cries, 'twas a confound Knock!
> While Saint declares 'tis all a Joke,
> Says he, there ha'nt been such a Stroke
> As that I felt at first alone—
> It almost broke my Finger Bone.

Most poets perhaps do better than this by the age of twenty. But Nathaniel Tucker was, for all his years, very young and very inexperienced in everything except ambition. "Nature has blessed him," said Sister Bet, "with talents which may make him shine in life, and the goodness of his heart renders those qualities still more valuable."

II

CHARLESTON

Do not . . . suppose that I make myself wretched because the means of subsistence in future are not secured to me. I should have as good a gusto for the blessings of independence as Mr. Anybody, but though they should be denied me I will not be unhappy if I can help it. I laugh at the world and all that are in it when I am in the humour, and when disposed to grumble I indulge myself in it.

NATHANIEL TUCKER TO ST. GEORGE TUCKER, 1773

CHARLESTON, the fourth city in British-America and the commercial capital of the South, spread itself complacently over the neck of land formed by the juncture of the Ashley and the Cooper rivers. It had been for years a busy mart of trade, and was destined soon to be even busier. Now, in 1771, something more than ten thousand people lived in its thirteen hundred houses, decently built of brick, or of white pine and cypress, neatly set along cobblestone streets which stretched back from the waterfront along the Ashley, most of them "encumbered with balconies and piazzas" so that after a day's work one might relax amid the breezes which swept from across the harbor. The New Exchange, the State House, and the Armory were all handsome edifices, but most distinctive was St. Michael's Church, whose classic spire rose almost two hundred feet and served as a landmark for incoming vessels.

It was a bustling small metropolis and seemed larger than it was because of a constant stream of transients, sailors stopping ashore while their ships unloaded, browned and booted men in from the plantations which stretched up the river beyond the city, or immigrants waiting for transportation inland. It was a gay center, much like London some people thought, with its theater and concerts, its open-air gardens, balls, and dancing assemblies, with its race tracks and cock fights, its taverns and coffeehouses where the traveler might find "a great resort of company as busy and noisy as was decent," where "cards, dice, the bottle and horses engross prodigious portions of time and attention."

When Nathaniel Tucker arrived in Charleston late in October of 1771, after "about ten days on the water," he was greatly impressed: "The colony seems to be in a very thriving way—the town encreasing daily, the inhabitants extremely free, hospitable to stran-

gers." Nor was the climate as unhealthful as he had expected—
from the point of view of a young doctor with a practice to build,
it seemed hardly unhealthy enough. His brother's medical business
was pitifully small, chiefly among Bermudians too poor to pay:
"The great number of practitioners made it difficult to fall immediately into business," and Thomas Tudor Tucker was a stranger
with "no connections to employ him, or friends to exert themselves
in his favor."

It became clear then, from the start, that the two Tuckers were
to have a difficult time. Thomas Tudor cordially welcomed his
younger brother, whose "good sense and truly amiable disposition
makes him the most agreeable companion. We shall, I am sure,
always be happy in each other, and although for his sake I wish
his stay here may not be long, yet I cannot help looking forward
with regret to the period of his departure." But the fledgling
physician would not have his family in Bermuda overconfident of
his ability immediately to wrest from medical practice in South
Carolina enough money to pay for Nathaniel's education abroad.
"Our business is at present almost nothing," he warned a few weeks
after his brother's arrival, "and I can't avoid sometimes feeling a
severe sensation from the reflection that our plan may possibly be
subverted." "Poor fellows!" said Brother Henry in impoverished
Bermuda. "I wish it was in my power to assist them."

But the Tuckers were young and optimistic, and held their
hopes bravely high, sure that "fortune in time will prove more
propitious." They lived simply meanwhile in a small house on
Tradd Street, "as happily as we can," Nathaniel explained, "under
the present situation of affairs." Rent seemed high, "a heavy
article," Nathaniel reported it, at fifty guineas a year. There were
only four rooms, two on a floor. "We are not much troubled with
furniture having in our parlor only three chairs and couple of looking glasses together with a few old prints of the ruins of Palmyra
and a table." Next to the parlor and facing the street was the
shop, ornamented with medicines and other necessary parapher-
nalia of the physician. In the rooms upstairs were "some old boxes
and a bedstead to which may be added my desk and press bed."
There was at least one Negro servant whom they had brought with
them from home. For a while they employed a housekeeper, a
widow from Bermuda, but she so ran up expenses that they soon
let her go. Theirs was a bachelors' snug establishment: "Rats and

mice have very little inducement to disturb us as we do not keep a great deal of cold victuals, seldom dining at home."

They seemed to have lived quietly for six months, satisfied with each other's company as they waited for business. But as time passed, Thomas Tudor became increasingly concerned about their future. "Our success here," he admitted, "is yet uncertain. I have no doubt of being able in a little time to make a subsistence, but whether more is to be executed I am not able to judge." Even he, who worried more than Nathaniel, still hoped that perhaps the situation might improve: "As yet we have scarcely had a fair trial, as the town has been pretty healthy since October." By spring of 1772, however, there was little change. "I am quite uneasy for Natty's sake," the older brother wrote, "as well as my own, for I am greatly afraid it will be much longer than could be wished before it will be in his power to prosecute the plan in which he has set out." The truth is, he acknowledged, "I have had little to do this month or six weeks past."

Money went out much faster than it came in, and debts seemed to mount daily. But young Nathaniel kept his own spirits high as he commented facetiously on their plight: "We must grin and bear it like philosophers of ancient times—and hope for better days." Like those philosophers of old, we too, he quipped, may "be obliged shortly to go without breeches and expose our naked backsides to the inclemency of the weather." Charleston was, indeed, a happy and a hospitable place, but "the people here are so uncivil as not to be sick at all in general, or if they are they take the liberty of dying without the assistance of a physician."

In spite of present hardships, Nathaniel did like Charleston as he first found it. "One might live here very agreeably," he explained, "had he money enough to spend, and if he has not, the hospitality of the inhabitants makes poverty more tolerable in this town than any others." To be sure, everything did seem to cost too much, or, as Nathaniel put it with more rhetorical effect, "Every necessary of life bears a most extravagant price, its luxuries are dearly found and in proportion." The only public amusement which appealed to him was the Dancing Assembly, and that was "established upon such an expensive footing that there is no going there, especially as a ticket is not to be procured occasionally, but you must subscribe for the whole season." He may have watched "the celebrated Mr. Saunders" who performed the puzzling feat of pulling "off his shirt without taking off either his coat or his waistcoat"—this in Mr. Stotherd's Long Room behind the Beef-Market, where the owner added to the entertainment by singing, and—so implies the notice of the performance—playing at the same time on the French horn and the guitar.   There were occasional concerts in Charleston, and good ones, arranged by the Orphæus Music Society. If one were settled and known in the community, he might sit with the Charleston Literary Society—to which neither Nathaniel nor his brother was, however, apparently invited—when it met in the library room on Union Street.

Yet even for a young man unrecognized by the community and without money there was occasional entertainment. Without doubt, it was a holiday excursion to one of the inland plantations which put Nathaniel in bed with "a tedious confinement for several weeks" because of "a soreness in one of his legs which he got bruised and excoriated by an accident in the country."   In April both brothers were proud, and not a little surprised, to be invited by the Right Honorable Lord Charles Greville Montague, the Governor of South Carolina, to attend an official ball on the twentieth of that month.   "He has been civil enough to send us an invitation, though we have neither of us any acquaintance with him," wrote Thomas Tudor.   Nathaniel as usual was more volatile and explicit:

The subject of conversation among the ladies at present is turned on a magnificent ball which is to be given by Lord Charles on Monday next at Pike's New Assembly Room.   There is much buying of gowns, alterations of head dresses etc., etc., that nothing can be like it.   My brother and I have an invitation and are to caper off accordingly.   The room is but lately finished and is one of the largest in America.   It is eighty or one hundred feet long, wide and high in full proportion.   I understand we are to have two sets of thirty couples each, both sets to dance at the same time as the room will admit of that or a much larger number of people.

He looked forward to the evening: "There will be such laboring and sweating I suppose at this warm season of the year that everybody will be sweated in their own grease."

The ladies of Charleston appealed to him.   They dressed "extremely gay," but they were "not very fair in general—I have seen no perfect beauties here but many very agreeable ladies."   Some of them, he noted with prim amusement, "drink grog and play at backgammon which appeared to me very droll at first, but I am now accustomed to it."   It might even be possible, he confided to St. George in Virginia, for an impecunious adventurer to improve his

situation by finding a bride among them: "There are some very
fine women in this town. But the mischief is that the greatest
toasts have no very considerable fortunes. There are many girls
with from two to three thousand guineas—but few larger fortunes."
Nevertheless, it certainly would be to one's advantage to keep his
eyes open.

Gallantry was a pleasant avocation, rewarding it itself to a man
of twenty-two. By summer Nathaniel had an opportunity publicly
to champion the ladies of Charleston, when someone who signed
himself "Eleazer" published a diatribe in the *South-Carolina
Gazette* in which he charged that "our daughters have waxed wan-
ton, and thirsteth after vanity. . . . If their grand-fathers or their
grand-mothers were now to arise from the dead, how would they
be astonished to see their posterity so altered from their day?"
Nathaniel thought it a "stupid and rather scurrilous performance,"
written with ill grace and great pomposity. He set himself immediately to composing a reply:

> How cou'd thy sacrilegious Paper dare
> To cast such gross Reflections on the Fair?

Seventy-six lines in couplets streamed from his pen as he turned it
upon the "mistaken, vain abuser of the quill" who dared assault,
and with such lack of chivalry, the costume and manners of modern maidens. Should they, in these days when men are "no longer
by tradition swayed," be bound to fashions inherited from the past?

> Shou'd Fancy, cherish'd by the blooming Maid,
> In new Commodes or Tippets be display'd,
> And the gay Beauties of our modern days,
> Presume to change the fashion of their Stays;
> Consulting Health, Conveniency and Ease,
> Less lightly lac'd, no less expect to please?

When Nathaniel had his poem printed, over the signature of
"Philalethes" in the *Gazette* of July 9, 1772, he explained that it
was not so much his opponent's subject "as the wretchedness of
the performance and the impropriety with which he attacks the
gay part of town" which had induced him to write in reply.
"Though thy intent," he explained,

> were worthy of Applause,
> Too mean thy Talents to support the Cause.

And there perhaps Nathaniel let down his guard, to leave himself
vulnerable, for one today discovers little to choose in originality

or forcefulness between the distorted, scriptural prose in which "Eleazer" wrote and the conventional, cliché-adorned couplets in which "Philalethes" answered him. Modeled on the more cleanly chiseled epigrammatic manner of Pope, in the popular literary fashion of young men of wit who enjoyed the intellectual exercise of wrenching a rhyme into place, Nathaniel's verses were sprightly and skilfully turned, certainly effective, if not as poetry, as argument. There was probably no reader in Charleston who recognized the irony of attacking, as Nathaniel did, the tradition-ridden notions of "Eleazer" on modern female fashions through the medium of verses exactly as old-fashioned and conventional as the tightly laced stays they deprecated.

The mood for making verses had settled heavily on Nathaniel since his arrival in Charleston—perhaps because there was so little else for him to do. "I have composed some little things since I have been here," he confided to St. George, "but none in the amorous style." An attack on the Governor (we suspect of South Carolina, though it may have been the Governor of Bermuda) was committed to flames because of its "incorrectness and unfinished state." But a long poem on his native island, over which he had worked lovingly and which he called *The Bermudian*, was completed by the early part of July and sent to brother Henry for criticism.

"I have spent some of my time unprofitably," Nathanial apologized, "in a fruitless attention to the Muses." It seemed clear to him that such impractical things must be put aside: "I must relinquish the thoughts of them and fix my studies upon something which is likely to be attended with more solid advantages than the cultivation of the Pierian goddesses. The genius of Œsculapius beckons me. I must not disregard the summons, but endeavor by making some proficiency in the healing art to cure at once the diseases of others and that poverty (I had almost called it the worst of all maladies) which attends myself."

As he considered the situation in which he found himself and the waste of his talents, he sank deep into disappointment, not untinged with self-pity: "My evil destiny has led me to a place where, I fear, it will be my fate to languish unnoticed without the means of procuring a subsistence." He and Thomas Tudor were "both very well in health, but exceedingly poor in purse, and God knows whether we shall ever be otherwise, or whether we shall not be obliged, if we escape a jail, to quit this place in a very short time. I assure you, I don't know what to think of it." Even "the difficulties of getting bread from day to day are almost insuperable, and they seem to be constantly increasing. Borrowing is and has been for some time our only resource."

Study abroad now seemed out of the question. Thomas Tudor, "from whose tenderness I might expect every thing in his power, is at present far from being in a condition to support me in Edinburgh or even himself here." For a while during the sultry summer months business did pick up, Thomas Tudor even treating a mysterious *"unknown foreign lady,* who has lately made such a noise on the continent." He and all the family, whom he made haste to inform of the conquest, wished they knew more about her: "The curiosity of some of the female part of the family is greatly excited," wrote brother Henry. But practice was still, after almost a year, largely among the poor Bermudians in Charleston. The town was "almost overrun" with them, said Nathaniel, "many of whom I am ashamed of."

Meanwhile young St. George, a student at the College of William and Mary in Virginia, was anxious to see the poem of which Nathaniel had written him. Brother Henry in Bermuda promised to have it transcribed and forwarded as soon as possible: "You must restrain your curiosity." When it did arrive, the youngest brother was charmed. He showed the manuscript proudly among his friends in Williamsburg and had copies made to send to others. His enthusiasm brought stern reprimand from his father: "I am told you have made this [the poem] very public especially to some of a low class such as Mother Jacobs' Henry; surely you don't set a proper value on your acquaintance to make such a one your confidant. Civility should be shown to every one, but we should be choice in our intimates, besides Natty I believe did not intend for anything but the private amusement of his family. I don't suppose you'll be intrusted with any more of his performances unless you promise to keep them to yourself."

The Tucker brothers in South Carolina, however, were overjoyed with St. George's enthusiasm. "I am glad to find that Natty's poem was so much admired in Virginia," wrote Thomas Tudor. "The taste in this country," he apologized of Charleston, "is not so well adapted in general to the enjoyment of poetical habits. Those, however, who have seen it, are well pleased with the performance." Nathaniel himself at once sent St. George a package of all his other poetry—"The Epistle to Eleazer," a long "vision" celebrating the

joys of solitude which he tentatively called "The Hermit" ("I do
not think [it] . . . worth your perusal—but Brother Tommy has
persuaded me to send it to you. It was written long ago. . . .   I
hold it much inferior to *The Bermudian*"), and a handful of minor
verses, odes, epistles, and *jeux d'esprit:* "You'll have poetry enough
to make you sick a month."

As we thumb through the paper-bound notebook in which today the minor juvenilia of Nathaniel Tucker are preserved, we cannot be certain which verses belong to this period, which were
written earlier in Bermuda, or which belong to a later phase of his
literary career. He mentions to St. George several "small addi-
tions" to *The Bermudian* "in the nature of those I now enclose for
your amusement. Let me know how you like them and whether
the characters are so marked as that you can distinguish for whom
they are meant." These are apparently not preserved, at least they
do not seem presently identifiable. There is a ninety-two-line
satirical "Epistle to ————," fulminating against some "pilfering
wretch" who had attempted to pass some of Nathaniel's lines off
as his own, possibly an offshoot of some small literary quarrel in
Charleston, not even important enough to have reached the newspapers. More characteristic of the gallantly whimsical young poet
is the "Jeu d'Esprit" addressed to "sleeping beauties" (perhaps his
sisters) whose absence keeps their admirers in black and hungry
despair:

> Ah, quit the Pillow, deign to rise,
>   And bid our Sorrows all abate
> Descend and bless our longing Eyes
>   Nor let the Breakfast longer wait.

Quite the most musical of these minor pieces is that "On Miss
Christy," an unidentified maiden who deserves to be better known:

> While desp'rate Lovers whine and sigh
> Their Passions tell and swear they'll die
>   With souls both dark and misty,
> Let me in chearful Strains declare
> The Praise of that unrivall'd Fair
>   The Charming Betsey Christie.
>
> No sweeter Lips were ever prest
> Than yours—With Rapture 'tis confest
>   By all that ever kist ye—
> No Eyes with equal Lustre shine
> No Cheek with Colour glows like thine,
>   My charming Betsey Christie.

Let envious Beauties, who in vain
Decry the charms they can't attain
    Attempt to turn and twist ye—
I'm sure there's none a fault can find
Or in the Person or the Mind
    Of Charming Betsy Christie.

The Natives of each foreign Shore
Need but see you and adore
    Their Hearts can not resist ye
Thrice happy he who wins the Lass!
In endless Joys his days shall pass
    With Charming Betsy Christie.

Such things as this were playful exercises, almost the result of
social obligation, safeguards perhaps which insured a proper end-
ing to a flirtatious afternoon with young ladies. It was *The Bermudian* over which Nathaniel was most serious. He invited suggestions for its improvement from the collegians at Williamsburg.
St. George thought that the title should be changed to *Bermuda*,
"one which occurred to me at first," Nathaniel explained in reply,
"but which was rejected on account of its promising too much and
misrepresenting my intention which was not by any means to give
a full and perfect description of the island."

The more he talked of poetry and the possibility, even for him,
of a literary career, the more dissatisfied Nathaniel became with
Charleston. His ambition fed lustily on the praise received from
St. George and his friends in Virginia. The Rev. Samuel Henley,
onetime Professor of Moral Philosophy at the College of William
and Mary, had not only suggested improvements to the poem but
had composed a sonnet in its praise:

Ingenuous Youth, whose oaten Pipe essays,
    Ere Manhood's Honours on thy Lip appear,
A Theme unsung since Waller's tuneful Days,
    Nought blush this Wreath, wove by the Muse, to wear.

For ill, with thine, may Waller's Verse compare;
    Smiling, to thee he'd yield the votive Bays,
And own how little worth his frolick Lays,
    The Meed of thy more happy Song to share.

Still range the Isle where genial Summer reigns,
    Paint the bold Charms that fire the glowing Eye;
So shall we find adorn thy future Strains
    Transcripts from Nature, that may more than vie
    With all the Day-Dreams Fancy can descry,
In raptur'd Visions, o'er th' Elysian Plains.

More than that, James Madison, just appointed Professor of Natural
Philosophy and Mathematics at the college, had written a long, four-
page appreciation in verse, "An Ode—Mr. N. T. on Reading Some
Poems of His," which Nathaniel with good reason cherished:

> To teach the moral song to flow
> In Numbers nobly great and slow;
> To rise the Friend to Virtue's Cause
> And stand the Champion of her Laws;
> To still [each] Envy's lisping Tongue
> And guard the wounded heart from wrong;
> . . . .
> To mount aloft on Genius Wing,
> And dare the Ways of God to sing,
> Be thine O Youth.
>   Hark! from afar
> The deep mouth'd Trump of Fame I hear.

"It is extremely pleasing to me," Nathaniel admitted to his
brother, "to have acquired in some measure the approbation of
some of the literati of Virginia although it is my misfortune not
to be upon a footing of intimacy with any of those of the province
in which I reside." He longed now, romantically, and with great
youthful sincerity, for appreciation. "Happy should I be, if fixed
in some spot with the means of procuring bread and blessed with
the society of a few with whom poverty would not be a reproach."
There he "might be permitted in obscurity to cultivate the Muses
at leisure, undisturbed by the glare of superior splendor or the
sneer of fortunate arrogance." He admitted that his reception in
Charleston had much to do with his present attitude. "Indeed,"
he acknowledged, "if we listen to the voice of reason we shall be
convinced that in a strange country where we are neither known
nor recommended we have not a right to expect that intimate kind
of cordiality and attention which, on our first setting out in life,
we fondly hope to meet with."

As we look back over the years at Nathaniel Tucker, he may
seem to us a little smug, certainly a spoiled and self-centered young
man, expecting too quickly a return for what he had to offer. But
from his point of view, there in Charleston, lonely and unhappy
in 1773, it seemed perfectly clear to him that poverty lay at the
root of all his trouble, his lack of position and his failure to be
recognized in South Carolina as a man of talent. Consider, he
said, those men "whose fortunes are ample and connections exten-

sive." They are treated with deference: "They live but to be courted and speak but to gain applause. Their genius is ripened and becomes luxuriant in the sunshine of prosperity, and they are considered as prodigies by the gazing multitude below." How different was Nathaniel's own situation, "whose niggard fortune obliged him to move in an inferior sphere": "His attempts to recommend himself are considered as the effects of forwardness and are discouraged by the frown of contempt. His wit is impertinent and his talents sink because he has not that consequence which should entitle him to partiality. His soul is chilled by the keen blast of adversity and the gripe of poverty causes his imagination to shrink." What then to do? "Let us," suggested Nathaniel with ambitious piety, "by perseverance and application to the study of our several professions endeavor to acquire that wealth which cannot fail to give us weight in the opinion of our fellow creatures."

During the summer of 1773 Nathaniel visited St. George at Williamsburg. The two brothers spent the latter part of July together, from the nineteenth to the thirtieth. "How blessed the days," St. George remembered them, "in happy converse spent." In Virginia, Nathaniel met all the people of whom he had formerly only heard—Professor Madison, Beverley Randolph, one of St. George's closest friends, and James Innes, a tremendous young man whom they called "the Major" because of his size—friends, said Nathaniel, "who by acquaintance of a day had more warmly engaged my affections than hundreds of other men during an intercourse of years." Letters between them for months afterwards were filled with reminiscences of good times in what Nathaniel called "that glorious land of disinterested hospitality," until the young poet set off for a short stay in Bermuda before returning to South Carolina.

When he returned to Charleston late in August, Nathaniel found Thomas Tudor up to his chin in trouble, as a physician and as a man of honor. He had been publicly reprimanded, accused of professional carelessness, of endangering the public health, and he had reacted hotly, to his own disadvantage. It started on August 3, 1773, when a person who signed himself "Benevolus" inserted the following notice in the *South-Carolina Gazette and Country Journal:*

SMALL-POX has not only made its appearance . . . but also . . . a Negro Man with that Distemper, near its Crisis, upon him, was last Friday Afternoon, moved in an open Cart, from a House in Tradd-

Street through the most centrical and populous Part of this Town, while the Inhabitants were employed at their usual occupations, to one of the Wharves, and amidst enquiring Crowds, sent to Sullivan's Island; without the Attendance of any Person in a public Station or Character.

Thomas Tudor answered the criticism—for it was clearly directed against him—in the next issue of the *South Carolina Gazette,* on August 9. He explained that a Negro man attached to his establishment had been taken sick, with pains in his head and back accompanied by a fever. There had been some eruption on his face and hands, which the doctor first diagnosed as measles, until he learned that the Negro had already had that disease. He then inquired very carefully whether the man had been aboard any vessel in the harbor, whether he had recently had contact with strange Negroes, for the possibility of smallpox was now indicated. Further examination disclosed no pustules on any part of the body protected by clothing, so that Thomas Tudor decided the rash was nothing more than rather bad mosquito bites, and that smallpox was out of the question. But then, when the Negro became delirious and the pustules enlarged, Thomas Tudor grew anxious. He called three experienced colleagues in consultation. Though none could be positive, each suspected smallpox.

Then Dr. Tucker at once warned his neighbors and reported the case to Lieutenant-Governor Bull, who gave him an order to the Church Wardens for the removal of the stricken man to Sullivan's Island. Let Thomas Tudor continue the story in his own words:

With two of these Gentlemen I went in Quest of a Boat and a Cart; both of which we found great Difficulty to engage.—The Market Wharf, which was the nearest, being very public, it was thought proper to carry him to Prileau's Wharf, where the Boat happened to lie. These matters being settled by the Church-Wardens, farther Trouble from them was judged unnecessary, as it was my Intention, at any Rate, to see the Negro conveyed to a Place of Safety. When he arrived at the Wharf, I was in some Danger of being obliged to bring him back again or to leave him exposed to the Rain, whilst I should go again in Search of the Church-Wardens; for the People who had agreed with them to take him, upon further Consideration, refused to do it.—This was the second Boat that disappointed us; but luckily I found a third, in which there was but one Person, who undertook to carry him.

"As a member of the community," he continued, "I did not

only my duty, but more than was incumbent on me." He was willing to stake his professional reputation that he had taken proper
precautions to endanger no one. One inquisitive citizen, who
claimed to be a magistrate, did, he admitted, come "to my door,
and made a clamor about this matter, but did not offer to take the
management of it upon himself." This interloper had spoken without the "civility of a gentleman," and Thomas Tudor made it clear
that he had no use for him. As for "Benevolus,"

I am at a Loss to understand whether or not he means any Impeach-
ment of my Conduct.—If he does, let him explain himself, and
make known his real Name, and I shall take proper Notice of
him.—There are in every Country some Wretches, Strangers to the
Feelings of Humanity, or the Checks of Conscience, who are always
ready to suspect others of every Act of Villainy which their own
Baseness is capable of perpetrating. . . . Men of this Stamp, it is
to be hoped are but few, and of those few the greater Part Reptiles
too contemptible for Chastisement: But should such an one be
found to disgrace the Rank of Gentleman, he may be assured of
feeling, in the Manner he may Reasonably expect, the Resentment
of one whose Life is less dear to him than his Reputation.

For a month, then, the quarrel disturbed the newspapers of
Charleston, Dr. Tucker writing in the *South-Carolina Gazette*, his
opponents in the *South-Carolina Gazette and Country Journal*. On
August 17 "Benevolus" pretended surprise that Thomas Tudor was
offended; he suspected that perhaps the doctor was too ill-natured
and capricious to be a gentleman. At the same time the magistrate who had called at Thomas Tudor's door presented his side
of the incident:

Having about Five O'clock in the afternoon of Friday the 30th
Ult. been told that the Small-Pox had broke out at Doctor Tucker's, on a Negro, who was just going to be moved to the Pest-House,
and seeing nearly opposite Mr. Warham's Door, a Cart which I
understood was provided for that Purpose, I was making all Haste
I could to the Spot, when in crossing Church-Street, a Gentleman
of very respectable Character, to whom I took the liberty of sending a Servant with a Message on this Occasion, and having on my
coming up to him, communicated to him the alarming Intelligence
I had just received, requested he would associate with me, as a
Magistrate, in seeing the Negro moved, in such a manner as would
least endanger the Health of the Inhabitants of the Town, but that
Gentleman declining the Proposal on account of some previous
Engagement, I returned with utmost Expedition, and taking notice
that Mrs. Bampfeild's Chair with one of her Daughters, was going
up Tradd-Street, and must have necessarily passed very near the

Cart, wherein the infected Negro then lay, covered with a Blanket, I was a little detained in making the Negro turn the Horse, and go a different way; immediately after which, I discovered the Cart to be in Motion and Doctor Tucker walking by its Side, whom with the utmost Civility I addressed, in the Presence of Mr. Warham and Mr. Petrie, not as he asserts at *his Door*, which I find on Inquiry, to be to the westward of Mr. Warham's on the South-side of the Street, but opposite to Mr. Alexander Harvey's, in these words:—Doctor Tucker, are you moving a Negro with the Small Pox upon him, in the Day Time, in such a Manner as this: Where, for God's Sake, are you going to carry him? to which he answered, to one of the Wharves on the Bay: whereupon . . . I replied,—as a Magistrate, I desire you will take the Cart to Lamboll's Bridge, or White-Point, through the most unfrequented Parts of the Town: But as he then told me he had been to the *Governor*, and Was under *Direction of the Church-Wardens*, and I found he proceeded with the Cart while we were talking, I instantly quitted him without saying *one Syllable* more to him on the Subject; and made all Haste I could Home, to keep my Family out of the Way of the Infection, in Case the Cart should pass my Door, which it did immediately afterwards.

This nervous individual was named Robert Williams. He signed his name when he wrote to the paper, and he wasted no words in accusing Thomas Tudor of poor judgment, of having little conception of the trust the Church Wardens had put upon him to carry out the job with care. Dr. Tucker answered him at once, on August 25, apologizing to the public for being forced to bring the matter up again "to remove any groundless apprehensions of the disease being propagated, and to justify my conduct to the more deserving and respectable inhabitants of this town against the aspersions of the ungenerous and impertinent." He presented affidavits from John Vinyard, a breeches-maker, Thomas Hammett and Thomas Roybould, both tailors, that Mr. Williams had by word and tone criticized the Lieutenant-Governor for not having any public officer present, that Mr. Williams had "come to Dr. Tucker's gate, or very near it, before the cart in which the Negro was, began to move."

Williams countered on August 31, denying that he had come to Thomas Tudor's door, insisting that he had met him on the street when the carting was already in progress. To spike the doctor's guns he, too, presented affidavits, from Charles Warham and Edmund Petrie, both respectable citizens, and—best of all—from John Hull, who drove the cart in which the Negro was carried, all swearing that Mr. Williams did not sneer at the Lieutenant-Governor or anyone else, and that, if he did, there was no white person other than they near enough to hear him.

So it went on, with recrimination and name-calling on both sides, through the first week in September, at which time—or perhaps before—Thomas Tudor lost his temper completely. The story is carried on by Nathaniel, with a great deal of gusto and complete partisanship, as he reports to the family in Bermuda:

In an unpropitious hour did I leave Carolina and in it a friend to be harassed and disturbed by a combination of circumstances without the consolation of being able to pour his sorrow into my bosom. And thou, my trusty cane! how couldst thou, in the day of trouble, as well as thy unthinking master, desert the cause of thy patron and leave him to be insulted by the proud oppressor? Had we been present, exulting shouldst thou have graced his head. Thy master should have walked forth in the pride of his heart and woe to that arm that had been exalted against thee. With many a lusty stroke shouldst thou have bruised the hide of the insulting traitor, 'till thy repeated efforts had obliged him to sink under the weight of thine honest resentment.

This was, of course, bravado, the sword-twirling of one too late on the field of combat. Thomas Tudor had acted with more expedition. Finding, or suspecting, that Robert Williams and "Benevolus" were the same person, he sent—but let Nathaniel tell it—

Our little hero sent him a very spirited message in writing (for which, he is, if possible, become dearer to me than ever) requiring a Recantation under his own hand of all he had advanced in the papers in contradiction to the assertions of T.T.T., and in case he should decline with such a requisition, a defiance to meet him at an appointed time and place with swords and pistols and either attended by seconds or without them as should be agreeable to the challenged—at the same time pronouncing Williams (provided he should refuse to grant such satisfaction) a rascal, a liar and a coward.

These were strong words, and there was—as one "Publicola" pointed out in the *South-Carolina Gazette and Country Journal* on September 28—a statute in South Carolina which made "challenges to fight, either by sword or letter . . . punishable by fine and imprisonment." But the Tucker blood was aroused, and Thomas Tudor asked no quarter. Nor did Nathaniel, who was bravely explicit as he stood on the sidelines and wrote home about it.

"But who is this Williams? I'll tell you before I go any further"—
and what Nathaniel had to tell is greatly more detailed, and
greatly more libelous than any other record which survives of that
gentleman:

He is a practitioner of the law in Charleston, and though not remarkable as a good speaker, has been passed off as the best Chamber
council in this place. This I am surprised at, as I do not think his
writings betray either solidity of judgement or even a tolerable
acquaintance with his mother tongue. Add to this, that he is very
rich, having at interest 12000 guineas, besides being possessed of
other valuable property. But since the noise this affair has made
(for I know nothing of his character before except as a lawyer) I
have heard he has been guilty of many acts of meanness and shown
such a want of generosity as had made most people speak ill of him.

Soon Nathaniel, forgetting digression and bravado, came back
to the principal point, the fate of the challenge and its unhappy
results:

My brother begged the favor of Sam Legare to deliver the before
mentioned message. Legare accordingly waited on Williams and
after making an apology in a polite manner for being the bearer
of so disagreeable a message, read the first part of it, requiring a
recantation of his assertions. Here Williams stopped him, saying
he could guess at the rest and that he would not hear any more,
except the paper was delivered into his hands, as he should then
know how to act. This Legare refused to do unless he had consulted my brother, who then requested him to deliver the paper.
As soon as that was done, he [Williams] tore it to pieces and said,
"You see, Sir, with what indignity I treat Dr. Tucker, and as for
you, Mr. Legare, (with a sneer of insufferable insolence) I wish you
a better employment." Legare was so exasperated at this as to tell
him, he was sorry for having treated him as a gentleman, since he
found he did not deserve it—that he was a pitiful scoundrel and
deserved to be damned.

Rebuffed in his attempt to force a quarrel, Thomas Tudor took
more drastic measures that evening when, at the Coffee House, he
posted "in the most public part of the room" the following forth-
right announcement:

Robt. Williams Junr. Att^y. at Law is a Liar, a Rascal & a Coward—
whoever takes this down is desir'd to fix his own Name in its Place.
                              THOMAS TUDOR TUCKER

The next day Williams came to the Coffee House, tore down the
notice, and "then called for pen, ink and paper, but after writing
something which he immediately tore and put in his pocket, was

heard to say, that Dr. Tucker was not worth his notice, but that at four o'clock in the afternoon he would return then and post him in turn."

Nothing daunted, Thomas Tudor "at the appointed hour armed with an honest crabtree cudgel and (I think) a pair of pistols in his pockets, sallied forth to the Coffee House to meet the rascal, who was big enough to eat him for breakfast. The town knew it— everybody ran to see the fun—but no Williams appeared. After waiting for him from four o'clock till eight, my brother being credibly informed that the coward had skulked home, and being advised by many gentlemen to wait no longer for him, retired to his habitation."

Williams not only failed to appear, but he also brought suit against Dr. Tucker and had him indicted both for challenging him to a duel and for libel. He cleverly "picked up the pieces of the challenge which he had torn and so ingeniously pasted them together, that the writing is very legible." And he used this, scoffed Nathaniel, as evidence. Subpoenas were issued to all witnesses of the quarrel. Thomas Tudor was forced to call on friends to go bond for him. "I am afraid," Nathaniel worried, "we shall be obliged to pay costs of the suit but hope the fine will not be considerable." Altogether, Dr. Tucker's controversy

has made a great noise here and served to render him conspicuous. By many (and indeed generally) he is much applauded for his splendid behavior on the occasion; some who approve much his publications think however that by sending the challenge he carried the matter rather too far, as he had in the papers not only made such a defense of his conduct as had proved satisfactory to all considerate persons, but had even expressed himself in such a manner as might have extorted a private message of a similar nature from the other party, had he not been of a constitution too phlegmatic to resent an affront in the way which has usually been accepted by those who call themselves gentlemen.

Nathaniel wrote in detail to the family in Bermuda of the trial, of Thomas Tudor's difficulties in securing an attorney, because the most eminent men had already been employed by Lawyer Williams: "The men of law in this country support each other in such a manner," he explained, "that it is frequently difficult if not impracticable to sue them, or when sued to oppose their oppression." Attorney-General Sir Egerton Leigh, "a man of consummate abilities but of an abandoned moral character," headed the prosecution, assisted by John Rutledge, who Nathaniel thought was unhappy in appearing for Williams. For the defense, Thomas Tudor had been able to find only Edward Rutledge, "a young gentleman just returned from his studies." But the Tuckers were delighted with him: "His genius and talent for elocution will, in my opinion," said Nathaniel, "one day render him at least equally eminent if not superior to his brother."

Sir Egerton particularly angered Nathaniel, but delighted the spectators, by opening the prosecution with facetious remarks which played upon the proud defendant's middle name, observing "that the family of the Tudors were ever remarkable for their choleric disposition, that our great ancestor Harry the Eighth furnished an instance of it, that he would down men and monasteries and—many things that came in his way, that as to Queen Elizabeth, though we have no account of her proceeding frequently to manual operation, yet it was notorious that she was accustomed to breakfast on beefsteaks and porter, a circumstance indicating a robust constitution, which is most commonly attended by an impatience of supposed insults."

John Rutledge followed with a reading from Lord Bacon on the evils of dueling, and for the defense his brother spoke passionately with "Shakespeare's who steals my purse steals trash" as his text. There was, he said, "in every noble breast a spark of honor (and God forbid that it should ever be extinguished) which prompted its possessor to support an unblemished character, that if it sometimes carried men to too great lengths it was a glorious fault and was entitled to indulgence."

But the case was strong against Thomas Tudor, and the judges laid down a stern sentence—"everybody was surprised at its rigor." The defendant was fined £100 and sentenced to ten days in jail for sending a challenge, and £50 for publishing a libel against Williams. "The indignation with which this news was received by most people," said Nathaniel, "gave me a singular pleasure. Every tongue was employed to express for Williams the contempt he so justly merited." What a despicable person he seemed as, "callous to every impression of shame, he triumphed in his success. The man really behaves as if he thought himself a clever fellow, and far from being conscious of his infamy did not even know himself to be a rascal."

The better element in Charleston, on the other hand, seemed to rally to the support of the distressed young physician. "Many of them whom we scarcely knew expressed their approbation of our Bermudian's conduct, and offered themselves as the companions of his imprisonment." Such a generosity, however, proved unnecessary, for, when applied to in Thomas Tudor's behalf, Lieutenant-Governor Bull remitted the sentence of imprisonment and the fine for libel. When Williams sued again in the Court of Common Pleas (the first trial had been in the Court of Session), he was humiliated by being awarded a verdict of five shillings' damages and required to pay his own costs. He threatened to take the case even farther, to the Court of Chancery, but something—Thomas Tudor thought it because such cases were not cognizable there— deterred him. Nevertheless, even the first trial had been expensive, so much so that it seemed impossible now that Nathaniel ever would get to Edinburgh. "The lawyer's fees and court charges being added to the fine will bring our expenses on this occasion to about £320," he explained. "Had Williams got [his] hide well curried into the bargain, I should have reflected on the affair with more satisfaction."

Nathaniel had played the poet's part in the quarrel. "My fingers itch to attack him in the papers," he said of Williams, "but I am almost afraid, as he is so fond of writing that I should soon be tired of answering his performances." Nevertheless he did begin a satirical poem: "I have invoked the genius of the immortal Churchill and am now about it. . . . The chinking of rhymes has . . . made a confusion in my head." He called the poem "Paramythia, An Epistle to Eugenius," and six months later he was still working over it. It would be a complicated and devious thing, not openly addressed to Williams, "although his character with some other circumstances will be so marked in it as to strike every reader." The lawyer was pictured as Mundungus, a wretch, ungenerous, dishonest, avaricious, and hypocritical, a liar who had wronged the honest Eugenius. "I have bid the thunder roll at W—— and . . . have bawled out against him with the lungs of Hector."

But, after Thomas Tudor's unfortunate experience in the courts, Nathaniel was not at all sure he would ever publish the poem— even if he did finish it—"lest persecution should ensue and the partiality of our judges here . . . should encourage the scoundrel's persecutions." Nevertheless, he worked over the satire with care. It gave safe release to his anger during the trying weeks of the trials: "If it fails in severity it will not be for want of inclination on my side." But he never could complete it: "I am convinced," he explained to his brother, "I was not intended by nature for a satirist, because that kind of writing costs me more time and pains than any others."

He was exactly right. "Paramythia" as it comes down to us today in unfinished manuscript is dull, a furious but essentially a meaningless poem. Twenty foolscap pages of it were sent north to St. George, who preserved them carefully. It was admittedly written in anger: "I think a satire is very insipid unless it be remarkably severe." Yet even friends in Charleston could not follow all its devious meanings, and its most sharply barbed references—to Williams's rascality in real estate deals, for example—have little meaning at all to one not privy to Nathaniel's carefully hoarded bits of local gossip. Read today, the lines seem shoddily pretentious, puffed with bombast, the shrill notes of a young man who jumped up and down with excitement at the edge of a quarrel without ever daring to mix in where blows were being exchanged. "I believe I shall never write any thing more in that style," he admitted several months later, "as I find it the most difficult I have attempted and contrary to my nature."

III

POETRY FOR PROFIT

Should my writings meet with the encouragement and patronage of the public, I don't know whether it would not be an employment agreeable to my disposition (provided every other resource should fail) to fall upon some regular plan of publication, turn author and live in a garret.

NATHANIEL TUCKER TO ST. GEORGE TUCKER, 1773

THE BETTER we know him, the more we are convinced that Nathaniel never could get far enough outside himself to write effective satire. But he did want to be a poet. Therefore, as a result of the encouragement of his new friends in Virginia, he had meanwhile conceived a literary scheme perhaps more daringly optimistic than any ever dreamed in America before. If medical practice in South Carolina would not provide funds for his education abroad, he would turn to poetry—poetry for profit. And this in the American colonies in 1773, when even in Pennsylvania and cultivated New England it was admitted that "the muses in this young country are yet in their nonage," and when the market for poetry of any kind, especially home-grown poetry, was virtually nonexistent. Only Philip Freneau in New York and John Trumbull in Connecticut, young men of about Nathaniel's age, had conspicuously dared the field before him, and each with limited success and very little, if any, financial return. Nevertheless, he would publish *The Bermudian* and from the proceeds of its sale would travel to Edinburgh for professional study.

St. George in Virginia was enthusiastic about the project. He and his college-mates Beverley Randolph and James Innes began to circulate subscription papers among all their friends, resolved to push the venture quickly through. Two thousand copies of the poem would be printed under the supervision of the young men in Williamsburg. From there it would be distributed all through the colonies, particularly through those of the North, where booksellers and bookbuyers were perhaps more numerous. "I do not expect," Nathaniel warned from Charleston, "to sell more than two or three hundred copies here, though I cannot form any judgment of the matter, so that it will not be necessary for you to convey me more than that number provided you have any prospect of selling the rest in Virginia, Philadelphia and New York."

"If you can dispose of eight hundred in Virginia," he wrote further, "I should be in hopes that the remainder might be got off in the other parts of America without sending any to Europe." This was a canny precaution, suggested to him by Thomas Tudor, who, from his greater experience in worldly affairs, advised "not to send any copies of my American edition to England as he says the printers there would lay hold of it immediately they found it would answer, by which means I should be deprived of the advantage of another edition in case the work sells tolerably well." To avoid piracy, they would manage a completely separate edition abroad. Thomas Tudor made arrangements through his old teacher, Dr. Thomas Blacklock, a poet and littérateur of some renown in Edinburgh, to have the volume printed in that city, where printing was cheap, but with a London imprint because that seemed more respectable. "Thus," Nathaniel explained, "the property will be secured to me and, if it should answer, I will have it in my power, either to sell it or cause another impression of it to be made on my own account."

Two thousand copies would be printed in Scotland—these in addition to the two thousand in Virginia. Even if they should not all sell, Nathaniel was sure he could collect enough from the Edinburgh edition "to idemnify myself and pay the expense of both impressions." Then, proceeds from the volume printed in America would be all profit, and the young poet's future assured. He would embark for Scotland with his pockets full of solid coin and with some reputation on both continents as a man of letters. Medicine could thereafter provide the livelihood, and poetry the fame. "I am," he admitted, "impatient for the event."

Plans were rapidly made. Even before the first line of type was set, the brothers were talking excitedly of possibilities for a second edition, wondering where it could be least expensively printed, in America or abroad. Nathaniel worried already about the London reviewers: "I long to know how they will handle me." His letters to St. George were filled with excited plans and directions. He recommended that at least five hundred copies be sent to bookseller James Rivington in New York: "I imagine he would be as likely as anybody to sell it." He worried about the transportation of copies from Williamsburg to Charleston: "Send them to some person either in Philadelphia or New York (with a letter) to be transmitted to me, as we have almost every week opportunities from those places." Above all, "write upon the box containing them to recommend that they be kept dry." Thomas Tudor added the weight of his influence to spur on the collegians in Virginia: "I hope it will not be long before we get some account of the reception of Natty's publication." He was proud of his younger brother. "'Without partiality I think he has merit little, if at all, inferior to the most elegant English poets. His compositions, in my opinion, discover as correct a taste as any that I have read."

Nathaniel worked himself into an ecstasy of anticipation. He would give up all thought of medicine to devote himself entirely to literature. "The cacoethes scribendi has taken fast hold of me and I am afraid would be an obstacle to preferment even should fortune (which does not at present seem very likely) throw the means of it in my way." He would "turn author and live in a garret." Nothing would suit him better.

"I should not be confined to any particular spot of earth and whenever I got a little money might indulge my inclination for wandering. I might stay sometimes in Bermuda where I should spend nothing, and sometimes visit Virginia, the parent of Genius, without much expence, or occasionally take a trip to the other colonies. I should thus have an opportunity of cultivating an acquaintance with men of genius and might safely gratify my favorite penchant to reading and writing." Even financial worries were solved as he contemplated his future: "If my performances would sell at all it would bring in one hundred, one hundred and fifty, or perhaps sometimes two hundred guineas per annum."

So letter after letter was filled with ambitious planning. Was he expecting too much? He seems to hope St. George would tell him he was not: "I have no right to expect so much success." Nevertheless, it was pleasant to dream, to posture: "My schemes of ambition are fled and every spark of the passion extinguished in my breast. Immoderate wealth and splendor which was once the idol of my soul, I have learnt to hold in contempt and could be satisfied to sit down to some neat hermitage . . . and enjoy with [a] good-tempered girl, in simplest style, the real blessings of life."

Nevertheless, he and hard-headed Thomas Tudor went very carefully over what seemed to them the practical details of their plan, considering exactly how the income might be most appropriately utilized:

I have just had a very serious conversation with my brother on the subject of the prosecution of my studies in Edinburgh. He thinks if we would manage to raise £100 sterling by the American edition of *The Bermudian*, (for it will not be long before we shall know the fate of the Scotch impression) that sum, with the assistance of one hundred guineas which we might possibly be able to take up here on interest, would enable me to embark early in the spring for Edinburgh. If this could be brought about he would recommend that I should set off in April, as I might attend the botanical class and some others in the summer and have time to prepare myself for the winter lectures. The expence of passages with some others that would occur at first would render £200 sterling necessary for my support the first year, and as he has now a smaller family [the Bermudian housekeeper having been dismissed] and lives on a more frugal plan than formerly he thinks (if practice should encrease) he might perhaps be able, at the expiration of that time, to make me a remittance. It is to be hoped this might be effected; but if it could not, I should have nothing to do but return. And if circumstances should turn out equal to our wishes I might have an opportunity (before it is too late) of acquiring a profession to support me.

But, in spite of such occasional vacillation toward the practical, poetry now seems to have held Nathaniel completely in thrall. If the first volume was a success, he would then, as Thomas Tudor put it, "make trial of some other pieces, some of which I think at least equal to the Bermudian." Nathaniel himself thought that when a second edition was called for, he would also at that time send "The Hermit" to the press. So during these exciting months of conference and correspondence plans advanced much more quickly than they could be executed. Nathaniel seems fairly to have jumped up and down with excitement as he considered what the future might hold.

Copy for *The Bermudian* was sent to Edinburgh by the early fall of 1773. As far as the brothers in Charleston knew, it had gone directly to the printer, who would rush two thousand copies from his press "in order to try its success in Europe." Dr. Blacklock, reported Thomas Tudor, "speaks of it with the highest encomiums": the volume should do well, and advance its author's reputation. But St. George and his friends in Virginia were not pushing through their plans for publication as quickly as Nathaniel thought they might. He wrote frantically, and his letters never were answered as promptly as he wished. There was some matter of trouble with rascally printers, which St. George never explained very clearly, but which at one time had him on the verge of giving up the project entirely. Communication between Virginia and South Carolina was exasperatingly irregular, tantalizing in its slowness, and completely frustrating to the anxious poet in Charleston.

In November he wrote his younger brother, on the supposition that the Williamsburg edition was already printed: "Let me know as soon as possible what sum you are likely to raise . . . and what account of its success you can obtain from the booksellers to the northward to whom you have committed the sale of it. Should the matter wear a promising aspect and should you receive assurance that the poem would sell well, even though the money could not be collected before April, I might set off at that time provided there was a certainty of having it remitted to me in three or four months." But these months went on with no word at all from Virginia, until by February, 1774, Nathaniel became anxious and more than a little impatient: "Write me at any rate."

Meanwhile, relatives in Bermuda had been doing their share in promoting the volume. Brother-in-law Henry Tucker subscribed for one hundred copies for himself and his friends, and he offered to dispose of two hundred more among acquaintainces in the West Indies; one hundred copies would go to Dick Jennings at St. Eustacia, one hundred more to John Smith at Antigua. Even brother Henry, the most dignified and least literary of the four sons of Colonel Tucker, who alone among the brothers seems to have doubted the success of the undertaking, wished Nathaniel well and offered cautious assistance. "Whatever may at any time be in my power to do for you without a public expression of too great partiality, which a necessary delicacy obliges me . . . to avoid, I shall be happy in doing." Specifically, he would see that one hundred copies were sent to Barbados, and he would write influential friends there to insure the sale. Indeed, he wrote St. George, if the first impression "should stick in hand" in Virginia, at least four hundred copies could be distributed from Bermuda. This from brother Henry must have seemed a conservative estimate.

On March 14, 1774, a package from Scotland containing twelve copies of the Edinburgh edition of *The Bermudian* arrived in Charleston. What a handsome book it was! "We know nothing," explained Thomas Tudor, "of the reception it is likely to meet with in that part of the world, for (by some mistake, I suppose) I had no letter accompanying the packet . . . [but] I have not the least doubt of its doing great honor to the author." A copy was immediately sent to St. George in Virginia. Another went to brother Henry in Bermuda, who acknowledged it at once. "I must own myself charmed with the piece," he said. "Not a person of any tolerable discernment has seen it but is delighted with it and desirous of procuring one." He wished he had a hundred copies on hand to distribute among their island friends.

But as that month and then the next month rolled on, no word at all came from Virginia of the edition St. George was superintending there. Nathaniel was frantic. Commitments had been made which would have to be met. Four hundred copies were needed at once in Bermuda, three hundred more in South Carolina: "Let me know how the matter succeeds with you," he wrote hurriedly to Williamsburg. "I expected to have received them long ago." Even in Charleston where he had so few friends, "I have been plagued almost to death," he explained, "for a sight of the performance by numbers of people, some of whom were almost strangers to me." If more copies were available, he was sure they "would find a very speedy sale in this metropolis." Nathaniel was angry now and disappointed: "Pity I had not them already to give to the bookseller."

As he waited for word of the American edition, Nathaniel's letters became increasingly petulant. A month before he had written to St. George:

> I do not know to what cause to attribute your long silence. Methinks if you had the inclination you might some how or other have found the means of writing me. . . . I have been waiting with the greatest impatience in expectation of hearing from you. What could have been the cause of my disappointment? But I will not reproach you till I know how far you are culpable. For God's sake find out some way or other of conveying a line to me. I have scribbled to you so very often that I have nothing left to say.

He considered other poetic projects, but halfheartedly and without the will to finish any of them. When a mutual friend in Norfolk died as a result of wounds received in a duel, St. George asked his brother to compose an elegy on the sad affair. "I will comply with your proposal," Nathaniel answered, "if ever the Muse should vouchsafe to inspire me." He thought the death of their friend was "truly affecting" and worthy of furnishing "matter for a very good tragedy." He wished he "had time and easy circumstance" enough to attempt something on it "in the dramatic way."

He thought he might, indeed, write a very good play: "I believe I gave you some loose hints about the plan of a tragedy I had in embryo—but I shall never have respite enough, I fear, from things of this world to put it in execution." He was encouraged in his plan for composing a drama by Thomas Tudor, "to whom I have explained the outlines so far as I had regulated them in my mind, approved it mightily and wished me not to drop the undertaking altogether but prosecute it from time to time at my leisure. But to be finished in the manner I could wish it to come from my hands it would cost too much labour for one in my condition whose thoughts, instead of being employed in representing scenes of imaginary distress, must be engrossed by the occupation of striving to avert the fearful reality." Therefore, he put the play aside among his papers, where it seems to have remained for almost ten years before, as we shall see, he found either time or inspiration to complete it.

Then, late in April, six weeks after copies of the Edinburgh edition had arrived in Charleston, Nathaniel learned with dismay that his brother in Virginia had given up all plans for the American edition. An earlier letter had miscarried—or so St. George explained it, though he never did explain in any letter which survives exactly what the circumstances were which made him decide to drop the project. His father chided him later for having been naïve in trusting colonial printers, and there is an undercurrent of accusation implicit in his own apologies for delay, which sounds, however, to modern ears as if the collegian protested perhaps too much in covering up what might have been his, not the printer's failure. Nathaniel immediately reached for his pen to spur on the laggard brother. There were so many commitments! Copies were promised all through the West Indies, and Dr. Blacklock in Edinburgh had printed only one thousand copies, not two thousand as he had been instructed. Something had to be done.

It may have been the sight of the Edinburgh edition, a copy of which we remember Nathaniel had sent to St. George, which touched that young man's conscience, so that he finally overcame whatever difficulties beset him and sent the manuscript immediately to press. It may have been the quiet reprimand from Thomas Tudor (who wanted now to marry, except that "poverty is a bar between us and forbids me to tell you when you may call her sister") which finally brought apologies and action from the young man in Virginia: "I wish the Williamsburg edition had come out as early as we had expected. I am persuaded it would have sold well and might have been of service in enabling him to set out for Scotland. I am anxious about him as he is now losing much time which is of utmost importance to him."

The brothers in Charleston still felt the pinch of poverty, and Thomas Tudor was unashamedly outspoken now as he explained their situation and, by implication, the manner in which a successful sale of Nathaniel's volume might have relieved it:

I am still dependent on the generosity of friends for my daily sustenance: and when this state of wretchedness will end I can not foresee. God grant that you, my dear brother, may never experience any such difficulties as I have been constantly struggling with since I came to this place. I have been frequently for weeks without a single halfpenny at command, and plagued with perpetual duns for trifles that I am quite ashamed not to be able to pay. In this way I have held out to avoid the mortification of borrowing, until I could no longer procure upon credit so small a matter as a candle.

Finally, late in May, three hundred copies of the Virginia edition arrived in Charleston. Four hundred more were sent, at Nathaniel's request, direct to Bermuda. James Rivington in New York disappointed the young men by taking only one hundred and fifty. This left only one hundred and fifty more for distribution in Virginia, because St. George, much to his brother's chagrin, had also printed only a thousand copies. But this time the disappointment seems to have been less intense, for even Nathaniel's first fine frenzy of enthusiasm seems to have worn off. Thomas Tudor wrote at once to express a cautious hope that the volume might still, even at this late date, find sympathetic reception in South Carolina: "I am afraid, however, that the number will not be very great. Hitherto we have no reason to expect great matters, as not more than five or six" of the Edinburgh edition which had arrived in Charleston two months before "are yet sold. I could wish that the encouragement given to this piece were such as to enable Natty to set out for Scotland this summer."

Even the impetuous poet was himself subdued, almost chastened in comment. "At this moment . . . I can't give you any account of the figure our Bermudian is likely to cut in Charleston." He had made the mistake of lending copies of the earlier edition to friends who, having read it without payment, now seemed reluctant to pay cash for copies of their own. Even in Edinburgh the matter went slowly: "I don't flatter myself with hopes as there is nobody to promote the sale." Dr. Blacklock had sent copies "to each of the reviewers at my request. . . . It is probable their opinion will influence the sale."

Nor did the volume seem to go any better in Virginia. It was not until July 2, 1774, that the printers announced in the *Virginia Gazette* that the volume, described as "a poem by N. Tucker, Esquire of Bermuda," was "just published to be sold at the Post Office." There was plaintive demand in the notice inserted in the same paper one week later: "The Gentlemen who subscribed for THE BERMUDIAN are desired to apply at the Post Office for their Number of Copies, where they will please lodge the Money." The American colonies in that summer of 1774 were concerned with affairs which must have seemed to them greatly more important than poetry.

But now, though still as poverty-laden as he had ever been, Nathaniel was publicly a poet, with two impressions of his first small volume in hand. That printed in Edinburgh, probably in February, was by all odds the finer of the two. With some perhaps pardonable intent to mislead it was attributed to "London: Printed for the Author. Sold by T. Cadell in the Strand, and by W. Creech, Edinburgh." Nathaniel's name appeared in clear, large type on the title page, followed by pertinent quotations from Horace on love of native land and from Edmund Waller on Bermuda. On the next page was the Reverend Mr. Henley's laudatory sonnet "To the Author," and then the 332 lines of Nathaniel's poem were attractively spread in large, bright type over sixteen pages.

The Williamsburg edition, printed sometime late in April or early in May by Alexander Purdie and John Dixon, publishers of the *Virginia Gazette,* was neither so attractive nor so carefully done. "To begin with," said Nathaniel,

I think the paper very good as well as the type, but would not the size of the former had admitted a larger letter? Yet perhaps that was inconvenient or impracticable by want of proper types. Again, if two or four lines had been taken from each page in order to leave a handsomer margin at the top and bottom, would not the appearance have been more elegant? But these are things of little consequence and the only remarkable fault I find is that the column of verses is not sufficiently in the middle of the page by which means the margin on one part is made too narrow and on the other part a large space of blank paper is left which proves offensive to the eye.

This last, however, seemed "a fault which might with great ease, be removed in any future edition." Nathaniel could not resist slurringly contemptuous remarks about provincial printers. And someone had been careless in reading proof, so that the last page was marred with an unsightly errata list. For some reason neither the author's name nor the quotation from Waller appeared on the title page.

But even without Nathaniel's name on the title page the poem as issued in America was by no means anonymous. It was prefaced by a dedicatory letter not included in the Edinburgh edition, addressed "To Henry Tucker, Junior, Esq; of Bermuda," and signed "Your most affectionate Brother, N. Tucker." In it Nathaniel defended his "little poem" on four counts. First, it was an initial attempt, for him, in a new literary form, and "written at an early Period of Life." Second, he freely admitted that he was "in some Measure indebted to Doctor Goldsmith's Deserted Village": indeed, "several of the Thoughts are . . . borrowed from that pleasing Writer," though many others, he imagined, "were only suggested by a Similarity of Sentiment." He could not, of course, pretend to compete with so great a writer, but he did suppose "that a Performance of much less Merit than his might possibly meet with a favourable Reception." Third, as *The Bermudian* was "an American production, I flatter myself with some Expectation of Partiality from the Western World."

So far Nathaniel's apology was a decent avowal of inexperience and indebtedness, together with a not quite ingenuous appeal to an incipient American pride in native letters. His fourth defense, hidden away in the last sentence of the dedication, is perhaps, so far as Nathaniel the poet is concerned, most significant. He had dedicated his poem to the most unliterary of his three brothers, but to the one most likely to influence its distribution through the island colonies. That was simply good sense. In doing so he expressed a desire "for the Approbation of Men who, like you, know how to set a proper Value on a good Heart, though its Emotions may not be described in the most classical Language." On one level such a statement is indicative of a desire to produce a poem which will sell well among men of common sense with money enough to purchase the volume. On another level it may be simply an apology, a statement of good intention, an admission of inexperience and of an unpracticed artist's inability to maintain a classic standard. But, most importantly, though perhaps inadvertently, it is indicative of something fundamental to an understanding of Nathaniel—and along with him many of his verse-making contemporaries—as a man of letters.

The Bermudian, though we may quarrel with its apparent formlessness, was not haphazardly written. The apostrophe of seventy-four lines to "Bermuda, parent of my early days," does seem too long in relation to the total length of the poem, and, as Nathaniel himself recognized, may promise "more than it was in my power to perform." It led St. George astray when he first read the manuscript in 1773, to the point that he took it on himself to alter the title to *Bermuda* when he made copies for distribution among his friends. Nathaniel, we remember, had immediately set him straight, explaining that the title his brother proposed had occurred to him at first, "but . . . was rejected on account of its promising too much and misrepresenting my intention which was not by any means to give a full and perfect description of the island." He was explicit then on exactly what he did intend:

My plan was no more than this, to write something which might shew my attachment to my Bermuda friends. For this purpose I take the liberty of conveying myself to some hill from whence I might have a view of my native soil and paternal seat. It might not have been amiss to describe the scene which presented itself in a cursory manner, although the whole island did not fall under my observation. Thus the sight of my former habitation recalls to my memory the domestic happiness I once enjoyed there with some other little circumstances which are thrown in by way of variety and the Bermudian with all his partialities stands confessed.

As a descriptive and topographical poem, *The Bermudian* is well within the limits of English literary tradition. Its ancestry goes back through Goldsmith, Thomson, and Pope to Sir John Denham, whose *Cooper's Hill* in 1642 begat a numerous but not always admirable progeny. And *The Bermudian*, like most well-meaning eighteenth-century poems, is explicitly, even self-consciously didactic, mounting in climax to paternal words of advice offered, in this instance, to a young man away from the influences of home.

But between the two conventions, of description of a quiet rural scene for its own quiet sake and of moral purpose, runs a third current which was neither traditionally quite respectable nor, according to classic literary regulations, sound. *The Bermudian* does not pretend to present, like portions of Edmund Waller's lightly satirical "The Battle of the Summer Islands" or even like Philip Freneau's later, more objectively particularized "The Beauties of Santa Cruz," simply a detailed picture of an idyllic tropical scene. It touches almost incidentally on the joys of solitude, of simple living and high thinking, as if these were necessary items of literary etiquette which a literary aspirant could not afford entirely to neglect. It is at root a young man's poem, written in lonely retrospection, descriptive not of the island but of the exile.

The Bermudian, then, is too personal a poem to be satisfying to classical tastes. There is something in it of indecent exposure, of lonely self-revelation which brings the response, not of "poor young poet," but of "poor young man." It may even be so personal a poem that it has little meaning to any one not familiar with and sympathetic to the troubles of its twenty-four-year-old author— with the result that it has received only the most casual reference even in detailed histories of American literature. Perhaps its failure results from Nathaniel's lack of proper education, or of properly controlled imagination, of whatever it is which sets a man apart as a poet, the ability perhaps to sift experience so that from the personal one discovers some residue of the universal. Bermuda was a small island, beautiful in its languid and colorful tropic calm. Nathaniel Tucker was a young man filled with repressed yearnings for accomplishment. With these materials, his island, and his own unhappiness, he did perhaps as well as any man could.

Critical notices were slow in appearing, but when they did come, seemed worth waiting for. The *Monthly Review* in London found that the poem "indeed, bears the Mark of Juvenility, but it likewise evinces the promising Genius of the Writer; who, if he continues to Cultivate, with Ardour, his poetical Powers, will probably soon grow into considerable Favour with the Muses." The *Critical Review* for July liked it well enough, "notwithstanding a few blemishes which occur in some parts," for "he who is resolved to be displeased at every thing which is not excellent, will find little entertainment in reading." "If this be a juvenile performance, as is hinted . . . , we may expect pieces still more finished from the same author." Even the *Gentleman's Magazine* quoted from the poem at length, and praised cautiously:

The happy island of Bermuda . . . has here met with a native to celebrate her praises with all the enthusiasm which the *natale solum* usually inspires, and in numbers not unworthy of a much older son of Apollo. In particular, the picturesques ideas which rise in our poet's mind in his hour of absence, on recollecting the delightful scenery of his native land, discovers marks both of genius and sensibility.

Though Thomas Tudor found such things as this said about his younger brother "most satisfying," there was in reality little but the most perfunctory criticism to be found in such notices. Yet what of that? They were appreciative, and the appreciation came from England, the mother of poets. America, busied with other things, was quiet, except for an occasional reprinting, as in the *Virginia Gazette* of November 3, of excerpts from trans-Atlantic reviews; and this, we suspect, was as much in an effort to sell copies left on the printers' hands as for any other reason. The *Edinburgh Magazine*, perhaps because of Dr. Blacklock's influence, devoted rather more space to its notice:

This Sonnet has been sung before by Waller, in strains more warm and enthusiastic than seemed compatible with the Genius of that quaint and witty Poet. The Beauty, however, of the Scene, and the happy Temperature of the Climate, are sufficient to account for this Inspiration. Here we find a Poet in whom the Ardour of Youth, the Love of Nature, and the powerful Prepossession for his natural Soil, unite their conspiring Blaze, and animate his Strains with uncommon Force and Tenderness. It is, perhaps to be wished that an American Poet had enlivened his Descriptions with some of those violent Tempests which disturb both the Continent and the Islands; but as these occur less frequently in Bermuda, and are less compatible with the Genius of the Poem, we cannot wonder that they are omitted; and though this had been a real Fault, the Beauty of the Objects which he paints, the picturesque Manner in which they are delineated, the Propriety and Tenderness of his Sentiments, the Clearness, Force, and Pathos of his Expressions, the Sweetness, Harmony, and Dignity of his Versification, are sufficient to apologize for a Thousand Omissions. Upon the Whole, if this Poem meets with the Reception it deserves, the most sanguine Wishes of a partial Author can scarcely anticipate higher Honour or Success.

Friends continued to be kind, and more than kind, in appreciation. John Page of Williamsburg, who had helped St. George in the troublesome business of circulating subscription papers, preserved in his commonplace book a poem, attributed to a certain Mrs. Nicholas, "On Mr. Nathl. Tucker's Poem the Bermudian," which in its sweet praise must have expressed the attitude of many other readers of sensibility:

> Hail happy Land, much favour'd Isle!
> Where Health and Peace forever smile
> The best of Blessings Heaven bestows
> Above what Wealth or Grandeur knows—
> What tho' remote from pompous glare,

These seek not thy salubrious Air,
Fair Science loves thy cool retreat,
And in thy Shades the Muses meet—
Bermuda hail! tho' erst obscure
Thy Beauties now may all explore,
Thy fav'rite Son shall all engage
To view them in his glowing Page—
And O thou venerable Pair!
Who live to future Ages there,
I gratulate you tho' unknown,
Nor wish a greater Bliss my own,
Than in the Ev'ning of my Days
A Son like yours deserving Praise.

Even John Adams in New England liked the poem, though it was years later that he said so, and he thought then that St. George, not Nathaniel, had been the author. "The description of the enchanting island, and everything else . . . are proofs of a rich vein of poetry no less than of moral and social feeling without which human life would not be tolerable." Colonel Tucker in Bermuda was proud of his son, but, at the same time, practically matter of fact: "His poem has met with universal approbation and done him much honor though I fear little profit."

But for all such heart-warming commendation, Nathaniel continued to be miserable in Charleston, impatient to be away to new adventures abroad. He wrote to St. George in May: "My uncertainty in this respect as well as the improbability of collecting a sum which might authorize me to set out early in July (which is full late in the year) by our American edition, have almost left me destitute of any hopes of seeing Europe all next spring." He considered going to Scotland, even without funds, simply trusting to happenstance to see him through. Perhaps St. George might be able to collect something from recalcitrant Virginian subscribers. "Indeed if we could raise here at present a sum sufficient to carry me to Edinburgh, we might rely on the prospect of support from the Bermudian—but our circumstances have been so much embarrassed."

He could not, however, remain disheartened long, as he recalled with gratitude all the good friends in Williamsburg who had encouraged him in publication. "I must request you," he wrote St. George, "to offer them my thanks and that in the warmest manner." John Page, Robert Andrews, Samuel Henley, James Madison, Thomas Gwatkin, Beverley Randolph, James Innes, the Nelsons, a

Miss Blair, and the Misses Cockle were each singled out for special remembrance and regard: "Greet them all in my name," he told his brother, and, as for yourself, he continued, now in high good spirits, "be diligent and assiduous and leave to fate the rest. Be not discouraged by the appearance of difficulties but boldly resolve to surmount them. Once more I repeat to you, support your spirits that they may support you.

> Nothing but Mirth can conquer Fortune's spite,
> No sky is heavy if the heart be light.

If you contrive to make both ends meet with a prospect of better times, learn like the fox and *me* to despise that superfluity of wealth and grandness you cannot attain."

He particularly sent affectionate messages to one sprightly former associate at Williamsburg, whom he only identified as "the hero of the haunted castle"—messages of condolence on "being attacked at so early a period in life by that great enemy of our locomotive faculties the gout," but messages also of encouragement and advice: "Tell him he must get married (for while he lives single it will be impossible to prevent him from drinking bumpers to his Patsey) and live a regular life. Many men by adopting such prudential measures have been able to quell the tyrant's rage."

Nathaniel was leading slyly up to the recitation of another ambitious adventure of his own. Having tried poetry, he now attempted an older and a much better tested method of acquiring immediate financial independence. He would marry a wealthy wife. "You must know," he explained, "that upon the accession of a certain young lady of my acquaintance to a fortune of twelve thousand guineas by the death of the father, I became so excessively enamoured with her that I determined to make a proposal of a serious nature." He was not successful, but he nourished no ill feelings because of her rebuff: "She is a good girl." "Success in this scheme, my dear St. George, would have lifted me above the necessity of vending either poems or physic for subsistence and secured to me the tranquil cultivation of my favorite studies—and favorite amusements. It would have enabled me to hold out my hand for the assistance of my friends and to do many other things that would contribute to my felicity. But the fates would not permit it, and I endeavor to rest contented."

St. George, who was himself making brave assaults on the heart of a certain wealthy Miss Galloway in Philadelphia, painstakingly copied Nathaniel's account of his courtship, as a *jeu de'esprit*, we suppose, to pass about among his friends; and he titled it "A Bold Stroke for a Wife." It is a good story in its own right, and told with frank vigor which brings Nathaniel for a moment to life. As we read it below, each of us may be forgiven, we hope, if we refuse to play the historical Peeping Tom by dwelling upon the identity of each of the persons Nathaniel mentions. It is enough for us that they represent families which moved amid what he called the upper reaches of Charleston society, for, in love as in poetry, young Nathaniel aimed high.

Miss Ainslie's father, who died not long ago, after providing genteely for his widow (a daughter of the Earl of Cromartie), left to her the residue of his fortune. I became acquainted with the young lady about a twelve month ago at Mr. Wright's country seat, which is in their neighborhood, and as the two families were on a footing of great intimacy was in her company every day during the time of my residence there.

As she moves in the genteelest circle of acquaintance in the province and on the death of her father, which happened long after, became possessed of twelve thousand guineas, I thought it would be no bad scheme to make an attempt on her heart. After deliberating very seriously on the matter a long time, I at length communicated my thoughts to my brother, who approved my plan very much. He said that it had occurred to him that it would be a good match for me if I liked the lady, but from a point of delicacy he had avoided saying anything about it. As he had hopes of my success, we concluded on the affair and consulted about the plan of operations necessary to be adopted.

It was determined that I should borrow a horse the next day and set out on my expedition, as the splendor of her fortune made delay dangerous ["I was one of a half a dozen," Nathaniel wrote elsewhere, "who aspired to the honor of reaching her fortune through the medium of her sanctum sanctorum"]. Accordingly I rode to Lady Mary's country seat, which is about fifteen miles from town, but to my great mortification was informed that they had stayed at Mr. John Izard's since the death of Mr. Ainslie, and had set out but the day before with that gentleman's family for Charleston.

I was very politely received and indulged with a tete a tete with the young lady, whose conduct upon the occasion confirmed my opinion of her good sense, though at the same time, it convinced me of the fallacy of my hopes. Who but a madman under my circumstances would have thought of disputing the prize with five or six rivals of the genteelest connexions in the place, and who had an opportunity of stealing imperceptibly into her heart? But I had learnt from the old proverb that faint heart never won fair lady.

She thanked me very politely for the instance I had given of my attachment to her. She said there was no accounting for inclinations and that nothing was more common than for ladies to refuse one person and afterwards to make choice of another of inferior merit; that it was very possible (if she ever married) this might be the case with her; that things which chagrined us for the present very often proved conductive to our happiness in the end; and that perhaps there might be a day I should look with pleasure on my present disappointment.

After a long conversation, in the course of which she gave me to understand pretty clearly that I was not the man after her own heart, I made a bow and walked off, very much pleased with her behavior and as much dissatisfied with myself. I don't yet know who is the happy man. I shall leave a clear stage for the competitors.

Other plans were quickly made. *The Bermudian* was doing badly in Virginia, where St. George was hard put to collect subscription money; his bookseller, he told his brothers again, had basely deceived him. It was doing badly indeed in Charleston. "I believe," said Nathaniel, "not more than a dozen copies have been disposed of. This is the season when almost everybody is out of town." But he would go to Bermuda soon, and would take a package of the volumes there with him. "The little attention paid it here would put me quite out of conceit with it had it not in other places met with some marks of approbation from some in whose judgment I place greater confidence." He urged St. George to print a few more copies, "to try its success northward once more." He toyed with the idea of bringing out "The Hermit" at once, perhaps only in Edinburgh where sales seemed to go so much better.

"I live in hopes," he wrote St. George, "of embarking for Europe the next spring. How long it will be in my power to continue there, God only knows." He toyed with the idea of settling in Virginia, without a medical degree, after perhaps one year's study abroad, "settling myself in some country place in that province, where I should hope by reading and attention to practice to make up for the want of a regular education." Above all things, he would not continue longer in South Carolina, though Thomas Tudor had offered him a share in his practice there—"unless it should increase considerably it would scarcely be sufficient to support him alone." Besides, Nathaniel by this time was disillusioned completely by Charleston. "Nothing but my attachment to my brother would occasion me to think of settling in a country whose climate is so far from being desirable and whose inhabitants in their customs and manners do not altogether, according to my sentiments, pursue such a method as would contribute to the happiness of one of my disposition." Not even the women, he told his father now, were pretty.

Furthermore, Charleston was stirring with political activity which threatened further to prevent Nathaniel's scheme of getting to Europe: "The Boston Port Bill makes a great noise here. Everybody is turned politician. Spirited measures are talked of and it is conjectured that resolutions will be entered into for putting an entire stop to all exports and imports whatsoever. The storm seems to be gathering over America. God knows what will be the event."

Politics played no part in Nathaniel's plans. Early in July, 1774, he set sail for Bermuda, there to spend the summer months "in happy intercourse with my friends on my native rock." There he might find the quiet and comfort of which he dreamed. "Sick as I am of the bustle of the great world, you can't think, my dear St. George, how much pleasure I promise myself in this little excursion." Then he would sail for Europe in the spring. "I don't know anything that is likely to prevent me except the taking place of . . . a *Revolution* . . . but I dare say that, if at all, will not be adopted so suddenly as to prove an obstacle to my embarkation."

Even his quiet native island offered no sanctuary. "In Carolina I was every where pestered to death with politics, than which no subject is more hateful to me, nor am I better off in Bermuda." He wished Lord North "had been at the Devil" before such measures as had recently bothered the colonists "had entered into his noodle," and he quoted from Churchill to prove the poet exempt from mundane things like politics:

> No statesman e'er will find it worth his pains
> To tax our labours and excise our brains.
> Burthens like these vile earthly buildings bear,
> No tributes laid on castles in the air.

Nathaniel remained in Bermuda longer than he expected, building air castles perhaps, certainly accomplishing little in pursuit of his career either as a physician or a man of letters. He enjoyed a "constant round of pleasures," frolicking from one end of the island to another.

Not until March, 1775, do we hear from him in Charleston again. Thomas Tudor had married ("My Hester is now on my knee," he wrote ecstatically to his brother) in July, just a few days before the poet's departure, and Nathaniel carried pieces of the wedding cake with him to the family at Port Royal. St. George had visited Charleston two weeks later, disappointed to have missed Nathaniel but charmed with his new sister-in-law. He and Thomas Tudor talked seriously of their own plans and of Nathaniel, of Miss Galloway of Philadelphia, and of the coach and six in which St. George would travel when he next visited them, of the possibility that the youngest brother might set up legal practice in South Carolina, at least in Georgia. Not long afterwards, Thomas Tudor moved from the city to Dorchester, some twenty miles away, hoping that there practice might improve more profitable. "I don't like it," said cautious brother Henry in Bermuda, who wanted the family all together, "and wish he had come here."

But the three younger sons of Colonel Tucker were each eager for opportunities greater than Bermuda could offer. Nathaniel, in Charleston again by early spring, booked passage for London in May, 1775. He had brought some money with him from Bermuda— payment long due him, one letter suggests, for work done years before as clerk to the colonial Council. Thomas Tudor did all he could to borrow more for him in South Carolina. Even St. George was urged to collect everything he could from subscription arrears in Virginia. And finally Nathaniel set sail. How long he would manage to remain abroad, no one in the family dared guess. "I think Dame Fortune has declared herself an enemy to our family," wrote Colonel Tucker, "for however fickle she is in other respects she is constant in frustrating every scheme that we propose. However, let us retain our virtue and we shall triumph at last."

IV

MEDICINE—AND POETRY

All the people here are poets and poetesses—some of them very wretched ones. Everybody scribbles what nobody reads but the author.

NATHANIEL TUCKER TO ELIZABETH TUCKER, 1775

THE VOYAGE was short, somewhat tempestuous, but filled with good times which Nathaniel celebrated in doggerel, "in the style," he explained, "of the Bath Guide." He submitted his account to the *Weekly Magazine* in Edinburgh, where it appeared, signed "Timothy Clackit," on September 12. "The blockhead of a printer . . . notwithstanding I had prefixed a fictitious name was so stupid as to add my real one which he had learned by some means or other"— that is, the printer had ascribed the poem to "the Author of the Bermudian." None of the letters which Nathaniel must have written home on his arrival in London have survived; perhaps this rhymed epistle, "Mr. Clackit to His Brother Abroad," may serve in their place:

No language, dear brother, can ever explain
The dangers we met with and storms on the main.
So much were we plagu'd with a horrible rout,
Such tossing and rolling and tumbling about,
Such a grunting of pigs and a cackling of geese,
That we never cou'd swallow our victuals in peace.
We had hoisted our anchor, but had not got far,
By the pilot's direction in crossing the bar,
When a gust on a sudden descending amain,
With vollies of thunder and torrents of rain,
Came whistling, like mad, thro' the rigging and blocks,
And drove us within a hair's-breadth of the rocks.
The passengers gaz'd with amazement and wonder,
And the captain, whose voice was more harsh than the thunder,
Curs'd the boatswain and sailors in terms most uncivil,
And swore all the sails wou'd be blown to the devil.
Down tumbled the tables, the chairs had a fall,
Away went the dishes, spoons, ladles and all,
Pigs, turkies, and capons, provided for slaughter,
Were scrambling and kicking about in the water;
And, what with their racket, and that of the weather,
You'd thought earth and heaven were coming together.
So away we were hurl'd in a panic and fright,

Like a leaf in a hurricane, quite out of sight.
The ladies below, who were stun'd with the clatter,
But cou'd not conceive what the duce was the matter;
Amidst the confusion of swearing and bawling,
Laid hold of a post to prevent them from falling,
And there, with intense perserverance, held fast
Till the dangerous motion had ceas'd with the blast.
Says I to the captain, if this be the life
You lead here abroad in convulsions and strife;
If these be the rubbers you meet with at sea,
The devil may travel by water for me;
For, tho' stout are your men, and well-timber'd your bark is,
Egad, I'm alarm'd, I confess, for my carcase.

As soon as the whirlwind and bustle were over,
And the folk from their panic begun to recover,
The way to our favour in order for paving,
As our spirits were low, and our stomachs were craving,
The cook, in great haste, put some fowls and a ham on,
While Squirtum and I took a game at backgammon;
And Miss Jenny, to keep up her strength, and divert her,
Was amusing herself with some bisket and porter.
Young Squirtum, you know, who with us took a start
Cross the Atlantic to study the medical art,
And, I'm sure, without notice you never could pass
Miss Jenny Swig-porter, that beautiful lass.
These two, with your friend Mr. ——— and lady,
And others, whom doubtless you've heard of already,
Composing a party as large as could stow
In the roundhouse above, and the cabin below,
Went over to see (parrot, monkey, and all)
That wonderful city which London they call.
Our game was scarce ended, in which I was winner,
When the cook rung his bell, and gave notice of dinner.
A sound so inviting we joyfully heard,
So we all ran down stairs without saying a word;
And Miss Jenny, who lov'd to be funny and frisk it,
Left almost unfinish'd her porter and bisket.
But oh! my dear brother, what numbers can tell
The strange and most sorrowful chance that befel,
As soon as the victuals invaded our smell!
No doctor's prescription or medical potion
Could e'er have effected so strange an emotion
As was felt in our vessel by those that were in her,
From the motion at sea and the fumes of the dinner;
So before we had tasted a bit of the damper,
Away we were forc'd to the windows to scamper.
Where we fell in such violent fits of exstatics,
You'd have sworn we had swallow'd ten thousand emetics,

Such heaving, and groaning, and reaching came after,
Such blowing of noses and vollies of laughter,
That the captain, who sat at his dinner before us,
Could scarcely refrain from a part in the chorus.
I'm sure I was ne'er in a pickle so scurvy,
For I thought all my bowels were turn'd topsy-turvy;
But since I've been quiet, and taken some rest,
I can eat my allowance as well as the best,
And they all must confess, tho' I feed pretty hearty,
That I keep up my spirits and life of the party.
Miss Jenny and I, in the calmest of weather,
Sit sometimes with pleasure for whole hours together,
And scarcely can manage our laughter to check
By the tricks of the monkey that's chain'd upon deck,
Who never to tickle her fancy can fail,
When he turns topsy-turvy, or plays with his tail.

    Since here, my dear brother, I've little to do
But to eat, and to drink, and to scribble to you,
Whene'er to the latter my spirits incline,
I'll call for the paper, and write you a line;
But, in mean time, I'll conclude if you will,
For my verse is run out, and my letter stands still;
No god to inspire, no muses to back it—
So I rest your affectionate

                TIMOTHY CLACKIT.

After he landed in England, gay times continued. "So much has been said about London and indeed about this whole island of Great Britain," he apologized, "that I despair of being able to make any observations on either that would be new to you." The city was more murky than he had expected to find it, but there was lots to do and many American friends from Virginia to visit.

Nathaniel just missed seeing James Madison, then abroad making further preparations for his professorship at William and Mary, but he heard of him from other friends. "He was quite an antediluvian figure wearing a hat and coat such as were in fashion before the flood. You may be sure under such circumstances he did not fail to attract the general notice and admiration of all ranks of people whose curiosity could not fail to be excited by the appearance of so primeval a figure. However no persuasion could prevail on him to change his garb." Perhaps it was American homespun which the dogged Madison wore so proudly, as did many other Americans at home in defiance of importation taxes. In London it marked him out as a provincial, a colonial, and not ashamed of it. Nathaniel was resolved not to seem a stranger.

Without strong political feelings of any sort, he could enjoy mixing with Whig and Tory alike. St. George's former college-mate, Kit Watson, was there with his loyalist family which had fled from troubled times in America. The Reverend Samuel Henley, who had written with such admiration of *The Bermudian*, was there also, "remarkably well affected toward Americans" in spite of the charges of heresy against him which had filled Virginia papers only a year before. The clergyman thought John Page and other colonial patriots in Williamsburg had gone quite mad: "I at first understood him in a literal sense but have since learned that his political opinions alone have entitled him to that imputation with the fugitive." Then there was young David Stuart, also from William and Mary, who was "so metamorphosed," Nathaniel told St. George, "that you would scarcely know him. That once awkward, studious, scientific being has now modelled himself into a buck of the first magnitude." Robert Burton, another former Williamsburg collegian, was also in the city, and Thomas Gwatkin, formerly of the faculty, had recently arrived: "They say his health is much impaired and that he is in danger of making a journey to the land where they have no need of professors." "In short," Nathaniel admitted, "I was so far from being at a loss for acquaintances that I rather met with too many that I knew."

He especially enjoyed a glorious visit of "a week or more" in Yorkshire, arranged by another Virginian friend of St. George's, Colonel Fairfax. "Won't you envy me," Nathaniel boasted, "when I tell you that the Marquis of Rockingham, Lord Abington, Sir George Saville, Sir Rowland Wynne . . . were in the number." It was flattering to rub elbows so familiarly with such men of good name. "And yet, my dear St. George, notwithstanding their elevated fortunes and stations, I found them amazingly like other men." There he also saw the much-talked-about Omiah from Otaheite, a "noble savage" then the rage of sophisticated London society, who seemed to Nathaniel exactly to resemble a West Indian mulatto, so that it seemed "a little odd to see him so much noted by nobility and gentry." There also he dined one day with the wife of Sir Lawrence Dunlap, who was pleased enough with the young Bermudian to offer him letters to her friends in Edinburgh.

The journey overland to Scotland, probably some time in the late summer, was apparently without incident, though Nathaniel admitted, "I was in great danger of travelling the whole distance from London to Edinburgh with an ugly old maid of an authoress whom Mrs. Blacklock introduced to me by letter when she heard I was there.   But I managed to get off and for my sins got into a newly established vehicle, calculated for carrying three persons, two of which happened to be virgins whose birth ennobled the last century."

He was royally received by the Blacklocks.   "They are very kind to me," he wrote St. George, "and never better pleased than when engaged in conversation about my brother who still continues as great a favorite with them as ever."   Lodgings were found him not far from the college: "My room is a good one and as the house we live in is in the suburbs we have an agreeable fresh air and are removed from the filth and noisome smells of the city which is not unjustly called the most filthy in the world."   From his window, "mounted up above the clouds in my aerial habitation," he could look down, he said, "upon the little world and the little men in it with great contempt.   In this exalted situation I have a very extensive view of the city and environs of Edinburgh.   I see from my window part of Arthur's Seat, I say part of it for its summit is at this time inclosed in a cloud."

He thought Scotland a glorious country, just as he had at first found South Carolina glorious.   Nothing would be better than to live there always—"if I had a competency.   Every thing is conducted with ease and conveniency."   Even the climate was not so severe as he had been led to expect: "Although September is far advanced I have not yet had any inclination to suffer a fire in my room," and "this is the effect not of economy but choice for I should pay no more if I was to indulge in one throughout the year."   To one who had lived in America, the absence of trees in Scotland—or that part of it which he had yet seen—made the countryside "have a very odd appearance."   But the scenery from hilltop and castle was superb.

Here for the first time Nathaniel moved in a really literary atmosphere.   He wrote happily of his new acquaintances.   Everybody wrote, and no one seemed ashamed of writing.   Dr. Blacklock, though blind for many years, encouraged him to keep on with his own poetry, just as the well-intentioned doctor had earlier encouraged the scientific aspirations of the American Benjamin Rush, and was later to encourage Walter Scott and many other young men.   As lectures at the university would not immediately begin, Nathaniel employed his leisure with long letters home and busied himself with another poem, this time called "The Optimist," and

written in sober testimony of the uncertainty of his ambitions.   It
was "great mortification" to him, he said, and a "great misfortune
to be obliged to pay such laborious attention to a profession which
I abhor and which, after all, I may perhaps never obtain a title to
pursue."   For, he wrote disconsolately to Sister Bet, "no degree is
to be acquired hereafter but by such as have attended the classes
three years, and it is a matter of doubt with me whether I shan't
be obliged to return long before the expiration of that term.   This
reflexion is to me extremely discouraging."

He wrote his discouragement into "The Optimist," which
appeared over his initials in the *Weekly Magazine* on November
30, 1775.   The vanity of worldly joys, the scourge of poverty and
dread disease, and the comfort of resignation to the inevitable were
all woven into his poem in imitation of what he had read in Pope,
in Akenside, and many another, in strands frayed from his own
lonely and disappointed ambition.   Nothing perhaps better por-
trays the state of Nathaniel's mind, honestly aspiring to goodness
and success, beaten down but not ready yet to give over his literary
aspirations, than these couplets which have lain for a century and
a half undiscovered and, we suppose, unread in the pages of a
small Scottish magazine:

> The sun had now withdrawn his light,
> And silver Luna rul'd the night
> With fainter ray.—Each bird and beast,
> Fatigu'd with toil, had sank to rest,
> Unmindful of its cares and pain—
> All was asleep but watchful man.
> Within my breast new sorrows rose,
> And anxious thought forbad repose:
> Pensive I sought the neighb'ring shore
> Where lashing waves successive roar
> With solemn voice: the hollow sound
> With awe inspireth all around:
> Beneath a craggy rock I sat;
> My theme was man's uncertain state.
> "Ah, hapless wretch! (with grief I cry'd)
> "The sport of chance, the slave of pride,
> "The child of sorrow here below
> "And born to taste of ev'ry woe!
> "Man's prospects now serene appear,
> "In pleasure rolls the golden year,
> "In sweet repose his hours are spent,
> "And ev'ry object breathes content.
> "But hark! how vain are worldly joys!

"To-morrow's sun his hopes destroys,
"Dread poverty and pale disease
"With eager haste the victim seize;
"The unrelenting hand of death
"Deprives his dearest friend of breath,
"His tender babes with hunger pine:
"Forlorn he calls the pow'rs devine,
"Of heav'n in vain he asks relief,
"For heav'n unmov'd beholds his grief.
"The lilly's cloath'd, the raven's fed,
"But *man* in vain may beg for bread."

I ceas'd—while various thoughts distrest
My troubled mind I sunk to rest;
When lo! before my dazzled sight
A form appear'd divinely bright,
The solid rocks beneath him shook,
While Nature trembled at his look,
And thus he spoke: "Presumptious youth!
"Attentive hear the voice of truth,
"Nor let the mind of feeble man
"Attempt the works of God to scan:
"To mortal eyes it ne'er was given
"To read the dark decrees of Heaven.
"But know, whene'er affliction's rod
"Chastises the belov'd of God,
"And with misfortune plagues mankind,
"It serves to purify the mind:
"The loss of friends and worldly pelf
"Makes man consider well himself,
"Think what he is, and whence he came,
"And what his being's final aim.
"Alarm'd he casts around his eyes,
"He sees the wretched, hears their cries,
"His melted heart with grief o'erflows,
"He feels his own in others' woes.
"Sensations of a nobler kind
"Now elevate his purer mind,
"The poor his future riches share,
"And ev'ry being claims his care.
"Or should it be the will of Heav'n,
"Which takes the breath itself had giv'n,
"To call him from the stage of life
"Amidst calamities and strife,
"While all his feelings grief impart,
"And sorrows rend his broken heart,
"His unpolluted spirit flies
"Content and seeks its native skies.
"But mark! when first in golden ease

"His days were spent, himself to please
"Was all his care; in sensual joys
"He both his time and wealth employs,
"In plenty revels, while the poor
"With discontent depart his door.
"Who has not felt correction's rod
"Forgets his duty and his God:
"Thus worldly ills for ever tend
"To man's advantage in the end.
"Be patient—leave to Heav'n the rest,
"And know *whatever is, is best.*"

    The vision fled—and as he spoke,
Methought the distant thunder broke,
Then vanish'd from my sight away,
And sought the realms of endless day.

    Beneath its conventionalities of phrase and thought we may perhaps read in this poem something again of Nathaniel Tucker himself, something which leads us beyond our hasty first conclusion that he was merely conventional and imitative. He spoke the idiom of his time, of course, and he fumbled to clothe his own, very personal longings within the warmth of familiar, second-hand, and, of necessity, sometimes ill-fitting notions of men who had thought before him. His father's voice—"let us retain our virtue and we shall triumph at last"—is echoed here, as is the voice of Pope and many another rationalist who temporized that "whatever is, is right." Looking ahead, we may discover in this poem a forecast of Nathaniel's later, more complete acceptance of the soothing and quiet benison of religion, and come on hints, also, which even he was not yet ready to recognize, that, unlike others in his family, Nathaniel would not finally be able to accept "triumph at last" and in this world as the proper end of virtue. Now, lonely and distraught, cut off from the comfort of support and sympathy from his family, he still felt the necessity of making a place for himself, as his brothers were doing, which would be not unworthy of the Tucker name.

    Manifestly, as he saw or wished to see it, his quickest and most personally satisfying opportunity for success lay in literature and in literature alone. Medicine, he was certain, would supply at best only respectable security, only insurance that he might still be well thought of and useful if poetry should fail. So, during the late fall or early winter of 1775 he saw a second volume through the press.

    When he had first written from Charleston of the new poem

more than two years before, he called it "The Hermit" and spoke
deprecatingly of it as hardly worth his brother's reading. "It was
written," he explained to St. George at that time, "long ago. . . .
I hold it much inferior to *The Bermudian*." But by the fall of
1773 he was already toying with the thought of publishing it,
though under a new title, because "The Hermit," he thought, had
been used so often by so many poets before him. "I have concluded," he said, "to dubb it 'The Philosophical Anchoret, A
Poem.'" He could not, as he had first intended, call it "a tale" because that did not seem to "give it consequence enough since it is
equally applicable to a narrative in prose. At least," he temporized, "it should be called a poetical tale."

He had planned then to ask St. George to manage the publication of this poem, also in Williamsburg, to follow closely on *The
Bermudian*, so that proceeds from both might help with expenses
at medical school. But certain objections to the plan had arisen.
In the first place, he thought it might be improper, by which he
meant unwise, for both poems to "be given to the world at the
same time, for . . . it would be better to let the first have a run of
some months before the latter should make its appearance." He
also wondered whether it might not be better to wait until he had
arrived in Edinburgh, there more conveniently to "print such a
number of copies . . . as might have a prospect of selling both in
Britain and in America, by which means the superfluous expence
of attending two impressions (instead of one larger) might be
saved."

He was not quite sure that Americans could be counted on to
"subscribe so largely to an European as they would to an American
edition," but he concluded that the risk was worth taking and asked
St. George to circulate subscription papers at once: "It is my opinion that it would not be improper for you (provided it is agreeable
to you and approved) to open, as soon as convenient, a subscription
for it and leave approaching circumstances to determine us relative
to the time and place for impression."

Nathaniel admitted inexperience in practical details: "As the
performance is longer I suppose a larger price might reasonably be
expected. But this," he told St. George, "would be left to be determined by you." There seems never to have been any thought in
his mind, now or at any other time, that he might be imposing on
his relatives and his friends. It was taken for granted that any
Tucker would help another along the road toward success. "I shall

make no apology for being thus troublesome," he wrote, "as I am sure you would very readily do any thing of this kind that might be consistent with propriety, for my assistance."

This had been late in 1773, and months afterwards, in the spring of 1774, plans had progressed little farther, except that now Nathaniel seemed more certain that it would be "cheapest and most expeditious . . . to have it printed in Edinburgh." By that summer he definitely decided "that it would hardly be worth while to print it both in Europe and America. At least I imagine it would be much more legible and less expensive to have only one impression of it and that in Edinburgh to be dated in London as the other." He asked St. George again to busy himself with subscription papers in Virginia and to make some estimate, on the basis of sale of *The Bermudian* northward, on "how many we might reasonably expect to scatter in New York, Philadelphia and Boston." Henry Tucker in Bermuda would advise on sales there and in the West Indies. London reviews of *The Bermudian* should give some indication of how many could be disposed of abroad. "Thus," he said, "after receiving the necessary information from these several quarters, it will be no difficult matter to fix upon the precise number of copies to be printed which I will mention to Dr. Blacklock and request him to superintend the preparation, if I should not be there to do it myself."

But nothing seems to have been done until Nathaniel arrived in Edinburgh, and there is apparently no surviving record of American subscriptions to this second volume. When it appeared, sometime early in 1776, from the press of William Creech in Edinburgh, its title had been shortened to *The Anchoret: A Poem*, described discreetly as "By the Author of the Bermudian." Like the earlier volume, it hid provincial origins behind a respectable London imprint, this time "Printed for and sold by J. Murray, No. 32, Fleet Street." Yet, for all such careful planning, *The Anchoret* seems to have been little noticed. If mentioned at all by the London or Edinburgh reviewers, it was apparently in periodicals which elude modern searching. And it came out at just the wrong time for circulation in America, where it was virtually unknown, for few books passed from England to the rebellious colonies during the war years, and, certainly, even devoted brothers, each of whom was by now taking an active part in patriot affairs, would consider it improper to push the sale of a volume made in enemy lands.

Nor does *The Anchoret* perhaps deserve more than the briefest notice in passing. Its framework, as Nathaniel had promised, was narrative, but its purpose was unmistakably didactic. The theme, in which we may again read firm tracings of the young poet's own rankling discontent, is stated in the first four lines:

> Among mankind how few are known
> Who prize the worth that's not their own;
> Who dare be just to others too,
> And give to merit merit's due.

Then, after thirty-two lines of invocation to Envy and its "attendant train" of such unruly passions as Malice, Anger, Discontent, and Slander, young Honorio is introduced, young Honorio who, like Nathaniel, had

> left his native home
> To distant realms resolv'd to roam;

and who, losing his way one evening as he wandered through a forest dark, came upon a humble cot nestled against a fair mountain's side. There, before the cottage door, an old man knelt in prayer.

Nathaniel's own sincere young aspiration, which we may recognize again as fundamentally religious, is perhaps seldom more nakedly displayed than in the prayer which Honorio overhears. Nathaniel's own good will, his belief in simple virtues and simple living, and his assurance of personal immortality were more than poetic conventions, even if they were not of themselves sufficient for the creation of great poetry. But great poetry aside, the devout simplicity which he put into the mouth of his mountain hermit deserves our reading:

> All-wise Creator!   Essence pure!
> Whose mercy ever shall endure,
> O Spirit blest!   Eternal Light!
> Source of divine perfection bright!
> For ever lauded be thy Name,
> Whose hand prepar'd the starry frame,
> Before all time whose gracious will
> Has govern'd, and shall govern still;
> Who, still pursuing Mercy's plan,
> With blessings load thy creature Man;
> To thee be thanks for ever given
> Who reign supreme in highest heaven,
> Worthy by all to be ador'd!

Kind Parent! universal Lord!
All-pow'rful influence divine!
Be honour, praise, and glory thine!

From thy empyreal throne above
Send mortals peace and mutual love,
Convert the hearts of those that stray,
And bring them back to Virtue's way;
Regarding still the just and true,
In mercy spare the guilty few;
Leave not the innocent to fall,
And let thy pity be on all. . . .

But why is a hermit a hermit? What brought you, O reverend
sage, to dwell amid these solitudes? Honorio asked the question
after the older man with quiet dignity had offered the traveler a
traditionally simple repast of herbs and roots and pure lake water.

To whom the sage, in accents mild,
Attend, and you shall hear, my child.

His tale of woe then unfolds through twenty pages. As a young
man, he had loved the fair Arpasia, and she had loved him. But
Envy, Slander, and Malice had risen to smite her down, "to blast
the virgin's spotless fame," with false accusation, so that she died
beneath the weight of her despair. Bewildered and enraged, her
lover had turned with bitter imprecation against the God who could
permit so vile an injustice, until Arpasia, an angel now, appeared
before him in a dream to plead the consolation of forgiveness and
the effectiveness of virtue. So, to the woods he went, to live with
his sorrow in solitude:

O Happiness! thou golden dream!
The child of Hope's enliv'ning beam!
Delusive phantom at the best!
By all pursu'd by none possest!
To seek Content, the world, and you,
I bid my long, my last adieu.

There in the forest alone the hermit dwelt "far from the wiles
of crafty men," and he envied none his wealth nor his fame. *The
Anchoret* thus develops its philosophic intention, to discover amid
the dark tangle of cruelty displayed by man toward man some intelligent pattern which the virtuous might follow. Must one, like
the hermit, retreat from the world and all its contaminating influences, cut himself from contact with all other men, withdraw to
himself and his own moral self-sufficiency?

> Great God of Nature, is it so,
> Was man created but for wo?
> Must all the pleasure he can share
> Confirm and heighten his despair?

Nathaniel was repelled now with all the naïve buoyancy of youth from such a possibility. His was no waste land, nor were his fellows who inhabited it hollow men. They might be cruel and lustful men, but they knew, when they thought about it, and he knew with optimistic certainty, that each was part of the mysterious design which God had set upon the world, and that sometime— if not today, surely in some better tomorrow—the warped and twisted wreckage would be, must be, revealed as part of a rational scheme into which virtuous man fits harmoniously:

> Some future period in thy plan,
> Must justify thy ways to man.

Meanwhile, there was little that an intelligent being could do except wait with patience and what strength he could muster amid

> whatever toils or pains
> Thy gracious Providence ordains,
> . . . .
> Convinc'd, even while with grief deprest,
> That all thy kind decrees are best.

This was retreat surely, retreat to the comforting arms of faith, secure in knowledge, so well authenticated in literature and popular eighteenth-century theology, that the father of all Nature did know best and would reveal when he best saw fit the inscrutable riddle of his perfect universe. As Nathaniel considered the subject, now piously, now in revolt, his couplets, as even our few samples show, are a pastiche of sentiments often expressed and better expressed before. We may trace, if we wish, his reading in Milton, perhaps, and Pope, in Thomson certainly, and in many others who in the eighteenth century wrote of getting away from it all to some quiet spot where nothing intruded except what was pleasant to the poet.

Nathaniel, then, takes his place among a host of other very minor gloomy egoists of his time who, pressed by one present bewilderment or another, beat a melancholy retreat to fluently articulated dreams of simplicity. It is not necessary, though it is possible, to find beneath the conventionality of his literary pattern some strands of his own immature individuality. To him, certainly, really exiled now by war and hard pressed as ever financially, the world was out of joint. Even retreat (with or without the "good-natured girl" of whom he had written a few years before) was out of the question. He could not afford to be a hermit. As far as he was concerned, the world had to be faced on its own terms. All that remained to him was withdrawal to faith that somehow good would be the outcome of his own young ambition.

So much for the small turmoils which raged inside his head. But what he actually did during the next two years few records survive to tell. We are not even sure how long he remained in Edinburgh or whether he ever enrolled for any classes in the university there. Official records offer no clue, correspondence with America was virtually nonexistent during the years of the Revolution, and Nathaniel's letters to Bermuda have not survived. Not until the fall of 1778 do we hear from him again, when he wrote St. George to congratulate him on his marriage to the widow of Edmund Randolph, an heiress who brought the young Virginian both a family of three small boys and considerable holdings in land. Nathaniel envied his brother: "Whether it will be my good fortune to arrive at independence," he wrote dismally, "I cannot foresee. . . . Let me congratulate you, my dear brother, that you are likely to attain it with the most valuable of all earthly possessions, a loved and faithful bosom friend to participate [in] all the joys and sorrows of this chequered scene."

"As to what concerns myself," he continued, "I have but little to say. An academical life has but little variety in it." He had been graduated the year before at Leyden, and had published a thesis in Latin on the successive changes of the human body from one period of life to another. The title seems not uncharacteristic and must have fed and been fed by the romantic concern which Nathaniel shared with so many other thoughtful men of his time on the mutability, the inevitable decline and decay of man and all man's mundane works. Then, after a tour of Holland, Flanders, and part of France, he had arrived in London by way of Calais on October 1, 1777, and had spent the winter there "in pursuit," he said, "of such medical knowledge as I could obtain." He considered settling in Bermuda, but wondered whether he would find practice enough on the island to make the undertaking profitable. He asked St. George to advise him about remunerative possibilities in Virginia. He thought he might attend advanced classes at Edin-

burgh that winter, then cross the Atlantic in the spring—"unless,"
he added cautiously, "anything fortunate or otherwise should occur
to prevent me."

While in London, Nathaniel found time amid his medical
studies for an occasional burst of poetry. What he did in private
we have no way of knowing, though, because of his interest not
long afterwards in writing plays of his own, we suspect that the
theater may have engaged whatever time a person in his limited
circumstances could afford. At Drury Lane or Covent Garden he
may have seen *The School for Scandal*, which was repeated often
during that winter, as was the almost equally popular *The Busy
Body*, or *Cymbeline, Much Ado About Nothing*, or other adapta-
tions of Shakespeare then appearing. He must have read with
alarm and some dismay the news from America which told self-
confidently of British successes and which ridiculed the plight of
rebellious colonials.

Whatever Nathaniel did during these months in 1778 was
quietly done, amid friends, we suppose, as carefully moderate and
noncommittal on political matters as he. He found his eager way
into print apparently only once, in public correspondence with a
"fair incognita" who on Valentine's day sent him a versified
epistle which demanded verse from him in return. His answer
appeared in the *Morning Post* on February 25, fifty-one felicitous
lines which assured her that, whoever she was, white or brown, rich
or poor, "prudent fourscore or mad fifteen,"

> I am wholly thine,
> My lov'd,—my lovely Valentine!

> O cou'd I soar, like bards of old,
> Beyond all mortal daring bold,
> To that fam'd hill, a height sublime,
> Devoted to the God of Rhyme,
> . . . .
> There wou'd I,—spite of all the Nine,
> Pluck a fair sprig to deck thy shrine,
> My lov'd,—my lovely Valentine!

> But since, a mere, mere mortal, I
> Must never hope to soar so high,
> But clogg'd and fetter'd, tho' I try,
> Must always creep, and never fly;
> Instead of bays thy shrine to deck,
> Pluck'd at the hazard of my neck,
> Accept, O thou, thy sex's boast,
> These verses by the Morning Post, . . .

This was good fun, excellently good light verse, and perhaps not ill-advised good sense from a bachelor now turning twenty-eight. Some days later "Incognita's Answer" appeared anonymously in the *Post*:

> Hail, happy Youth! the fav'rite of the Nine,
> Whose music well would grace *Apollo's* shrine,
> Hail, happy Nymph! with such a *Valentine*!

But, as his third year away from America drew to a close, Nathaniel was still at loose ends. There seemed little opportunity of returning to South Carolina or Virginia, and even the voyage to Bermuda was more hazardous than it had been before. With some practical reservations, he was content with the prospect of remaining abroad indefinitely: "As the practice of physic in this country is easy and lucrative I have had thoughts of settling in some part of England, but have at present no prospect of bringing this about as it would not be prudent to attempt it, without some certain resource in case of need for the first two or three years when my income from my business would probably be small and my expenses no less than £150 or perhaps £200 per annum."

Perhaps his brothers might again suggest some means of financial assistance, for Nathaniel felt strongly now that life was rushing past him. "It is high time," he wrote lugubriously to St. George, "for me to think of taking root somewhere before I be blasted by the winter of life and the tender blossoms of hope and a flourishing season forever withered."

WAR—AND POETRY

Furnished, like Robinson Crusoe, on an unfrequented coast, with excellent materials but miserable tools, I have been occupied in constructing the bark in which I am to make my voyage over the ocean of time to the distant shore of posterity. Every man who engages in such an undertaking must make allowances for the danger of shipwreck and disappointment.

NATHANIEL TUCKER TO ST. GEORGE TUCKER, 1784

IN THE SPRING of 1779 Nathaniel set up as a practicing physician in the old town of Malton in Yorkshire with, he told his friends in Bermuda, "the fairest prospects for success." "He has had the good fortune," brother Henry reported to St. George, "to have been introduced to many people of the first rank and fashion in the vicinity" and had been "received with politeness and respect." Charles Watson Wentworth, Marquis of Rockingham, was particularly civil to the young doctor. "May heaven grant him all the success he deserves!" wrote Colonel Tucker. "He has fixed himself in a rich country, and must be unlucky indeed, if he fails to do well." Nonetheless, Henry Tucker sent Nathaniel fifty pounds to tide him over the first difficult months, and Thomas Tudor, remembering his own uncertain experience in Charleston, wondered whether that sum was indeed enough.

Some eighteen miles away was the fashionable spa of Scarborough, which, Nathaniel explained, was "much resorted to in summer and fall for the benefit of the waters and sea bathing by a very numerous and genteel company." He meant, we presume, that for a young physician's purposes it was a wealthy and potentially a profitable company. He expected to spend most of his time there during the popular season, picking up what prosperous patients he could; then during the slack winter months he would establish a more solid and permanent clientele among the less spectacular townspeople of Malton. During his first two years he seems to have been busy, if not with medical affairs, with something which engrossed his time. The family in Bermuda heard from him infrequently, and then only through Colonel Tucker, who was again in London as agent for the island colony and who reported that his son spoke "with cheerfulness of his prospects" and seemed, at last, well likely to make something of himself as a physician.

But as time went on and the struggle for practice lost perhaps some of its fresh novelty, Nathaniel seems increasingly to have felt his isolation from friends and family across the Atlantic. Letters came to him rarely now, even from Thomas Tudor and St. George, each of whom was busy in patriotic support of the Revolution, and each with a family of his own in America. Indeed, letters of any sort passed very slowly back and forth, when they passed at all. There was continuing suspicion that correspondence to the rebellious colonies was intercepted and read by agents of the Ministry, so that one could not speak his mind freely. Nathaniel wished he were not so cut off from home. He worried that the war stood between him and opportunities for success. He meant literary success, and he continued halfheartedly to compose, though he admitted that "the world in general, is too busy with its own affairs to spare time to read what I am fool enough to write."

Nevertheless, in 1783 he sent Sister Bet at Port Royal a package of poems, which she either did not receive or did not acknowledge as quickly as he thought proper. He followed with a petulant letter: "I always write to my friends. But they never write to me."

You are little acquainted with the vanity of an author if you think he can be satisfied with having his works passed over in silence and neglect by the only persons to whom they are communicated. I declare to you that the greatest and almost the only pleasure I have in composing is in thinking of the manner in which my dearest friends will be affected by what I produce. What will they say of this passage or the other? Will they commend or will they disapprove? What will their remarks be when this or that is read over in full assembly? . . . I do not require a formal dissertation fit for the press, but their undisguised sentiments to regulate my own taste in my future undertakings.

He thought of himself more than ever as a poet without an audience, and he missed the sympathetic encouragement he had always received from his family. "In composing," he pleaded, "my brains are so confused with turning and twisting and altering and scratching out and putting in that I cannot form the least idea of the effect any of my writings would produce when read by another." There certainly was no one in Malton to whom he could turn. "I have not a creature here to whom I can communicate anything. It is only to my friends beyond the sea that I can learn it." Not, he insisted, "that I am sick for applause, for I am fully as solicitous to be told of faults and imperfections as of any thing that might be deemed worthy of approbation."

Encouragement did come to him, and apparently just about this time, from an unexpected quarter, from England, and unsolicited, from an English poet who was not only widely known but who was also on intimate terms with most of the established literary men of that time. An aspiring writer could hardly hope for more in praise or appreciation than Nathaniel received now from Anna Seward, the "Swan of Lichfield," protégé of Erasmus Darwin, friend and confidant of William Hayley, and recognized by all readers of sensibility as one of the sweetest voices then raised in song. Beyond any doubt, she was a "celebrated person": she had known the great Dr. Johnson and she corresponded familiarly with many of his circle. Not long before, she had read *The Bermudian* and liked it so much that she wrote four pages of verse to Nathaniel to express her admiration of the poem and her good wishes to him for comparable success in his new pursuit of medicine:

> Thou, who 'midst lading suns and wayward skies
> Regretful bendest thy averted eyes
> Where, far extended in the ardent west
> Thy native island lifts her palmy breast,
> Accept the sympathies that rise sincere
> For each lost joy that prompts thy starting tear!
> . . . .
> May Science bless with clearest light thy youth
> And wisdom guide thee to the fane of truth!
> O'er vain regrets hope, love and joy prevail,
> Warm as Bermuda's sun and gentle as her gale!

Thrilled, we suppose, not only at the praise but in the knowledge that it came from so well-beloved an English poet, Nathaniel wrote twenty-five pages of blank verse in reply. Much of it was literary genuflexion to Miss Seward, her charm, her wit, her accomplishment, her taste, and Nathaniel's sorrow that he could not rise to her level. But it was impossible for him to write long without coming to himself, his hopes, and his disappointments. And on these subjects he managed better poetry than usual, reinforcing our certainty (and his own) that Nathaniel was unhappy.

> Him who of all this palm-island's sons
> Most lov'd her and most sought her secret conference
> Touch'd with the melody of heavenly song
> Yet now no more he courts her in these haunts
> Tho' lov'd as erst, but to far other climes
> Wandering inglorious, his neglected harp
> Untuneable there hung where still suspense

It rusts in the deep shade. Bird of the tropic
With streaming length of tail thro' liquid azure
Steering thy airy voyage, from these shores
Haply no more the loiterer shall pursue
With fixed eyes thy flight, sailing remote
Along the bosom of th' etherial sky
And lessening momentary until the ray
Of optic sense but paint thee as an atom
Floating amidst the grand celestial void:
For now he roams no more his native lands
But uncompell'd, in voluntary exile,
Explores the book of man, and various nations.
From the dark lanthorn of his own obscurity
Contemplates unobserv'd, searching their hearts
And reading on the tables of the front,
As in plain characters, the obscure lineaments
That marks the soul's complexion.

Voluntary or not, Nathaniel did think of himself as an exile and lonely, condemned to live among strangers and forced to make his living by means of a profession which he felt neither congenial nor quite worthy of his talents:

                    his daily steps
Bending assiduous to the darken'd room
Of groaning sickness, or in his retirement
Where the pale midnight lamp with trembling ray
Illumes the page of Science, tracing in silence
The windings of her unfrequented path.

How much better, this last pursuit, to strip the "tinsel trumpery," the "false glitter," and the "gay embroidery" from affectation,

                    seeking and studying
Truth uncontaminate and thro' her knowledge
Divine Philosophy to hear unruffled
On the rough road of life the tilts and jostlings
Of this rude world.

The young man was, of course, dramatizing himself. He was neither so good a poet, so devoted a native son, nor so conscientious a scientist as he made himself out to be. In our hurried summary of his literary aspirations and achievements we have, however, neither the room nor the temerity to attempt an analysis which goes very far behind his own simple statement that he wanted to be a poet, at least to live in the luxurious simplicity which he imagined a poet might find, but that he had to make his way in the world, and that medicine seemed to offer him the best path, though he did not like it and wished he might simply be a poet. By now we can anticipate his brothers and say, as they were to say, "poor Natty," even "poor, poor Natty."

The war in America troubled him, in conscience because he was not part of it, and, more deeply, because it tore to ugly pieces the world he dreamed of building about himself. He wrote with resentment of his inability to speak out in defense of American liberties. Situated as he was, dependent on Englishmen for his daily bread, it would have been neither greatly helpful nor wise to have committed himself. He was not a good quarreler—his experience in Charleston had taught him that. He was not adept in satire, even if it had been practical to produce satire dedicated to a cause unpopular with many of his Yorkshire neighbors. It certainly would not be good common sense for a young doctor to alienate patients, even prospective patients, by speaking his mind too sharply.

Yet the war was often on his mind, disturbing him and perplexing him, getting into his way and into the way of his career. It bred a "mighty chaos," he said in his reply to Miss Seward, "dreary and waste, come to confound the world." It even withered some of the charm of his native island, where

> the breath of war
> Most pestilential, in these later times,
> Hath sear'd her prosperous green and foul contagion
> Stain'd her pure air.

As war affected Bermuda and the fortunes of Bermudians, it affected him also, in spirit and in purse:

> Famine at large
> Roams on our coast and this unhappy isle
> Invades or threatens, a huge hidebound giantess
> Tenfold more hideous and deform than those
> Poets have fabled.

As an islander, bred to familiarity with the sea, Nathaniel's imagination particularly played upon the perils and excitement of naval warfare, where "squadrons thick to hostile squadrons" were opposed in battle, which each cannon from "brazen throat . . . outbelches,"

> infernal storm
> Of iron hail, black smoke and ruddy flame,
> . . . .
> Rains iron tempest from the hollow mouths

Of bellowing ordnance, vomiting severe
Chain shot and double headed, thick as hail
Hissing in air; not only where they hit
Driving out life with slaughter of whole ranks
Crush'd into fragments, but sweeping as they fly
Cordage, disabled yards and shiver'd masts.

He pictured hosts of stalwart men, "marines and mariners," glut-
ting the "ravenous maw" of the "ocean and its monsters,"

all in one instance
Blasted from life, their sum of glory finish'd.

Horrible in so many respects to a poet's sensitive brooding, the
American Revolution was nonetheless thrilling as a contemporary
instance of the triumph of an ideal, as "British thunder," said
Nathaniel, "shook, not subverted," the "tottering throne of Freedom in the west." As such it represented materials such as poets
had always been proud to fashion into song. Now, in 1783, as the
conflict seemed drawing to a close, perhaps he, too, might contribute
a poet's share by celebrating, not the details, of which he admittedly knew little, but the pulse-quickening promise of freedom for
all men of which the war in America seemed harbinger. Neither
the quick, probing wit of Pope nor the bludgeon attack of Churchill would suit him now. Turning rather to the majestic line of
Milton, he would write an epic which would preserve the memory
of the American Revolution in the minds of men forever. Such
a poem might be the bark, said Nathaniel, on which he, also, would
"voyage over the ocean of time to the distant shore of posterity."

He set himself immediately to the task. Composing rapidly,
he completed the first book during the summer of 1783 and started
on the second. The composition in its entirety would be called
America Delivered and would be properly described as "an heroic
poem." The first part, consisting of six long books, would have
its own title, "The Triumph of Patriotism, or the Defeat of Mammon." It flowed fast from his pen, an allegory in the grandest style,
in which the angels of Heaven and the demons of Hell contended
for control of man in America. Nathaniel charted his course in
six tight-written pages of prose explanation; then, after thirty-four
Miltonic lines of invocation to the Spirit of Liberty, he hastened—
the verb is his—to the midst of the action, wherein the reader is
introduced to the archangel Michael, "the celestial spirit of Wisdom," as he "shoots like a blazing star" from celestial realms to

Philadelphia, to give advice to the American Congress as it meets with British commissioners to consider terms for peace.

At the same time, however, infernal spirits "who occupy the adverse region the other side of Chaos" meet in evil conclave:

> There frightful forms appear'd
> Thronging the ways or riding thro' the air
> On leathern wings, dire hell-engender'd monsters
> Shaggy and vast, or cover'd o'er with scales
> As dragons, breathing fire, with glowing eyes
> That burn'd as lamps; part cloven-footed, arm'd
> With tail of mortal sting, horned and fang'd
> To torture and perplex.

Led by Satan, the spirit of Ambition, they plot the downfall of American liberty:

> Princes and potentates, illustrious founders
> And sovrans of this newly founded kingdom—

Like his Miltonic predecessor, Satan is addressing his assembled chief lieutenants, Beelzebub, Belial, Moloch, and Mammon, who speak, each in turn, much as they spoke in *Paradise Lost*, to suggest some evil means of perverting the good colonials. As a result of their deliberations, Mammon is dispatched to earth as Hell's representative best qualified to carry out their corrupt designs.

This is a far as Nathaniel had progressed when he sent a copy of the poem to Sister Bet in Bermuda, asking her candid opinion. Should he continue with it? Or had he attempted something too large for him? She replied in what seems today naïve understatement that the poem seemed to get started very slowly, that it was weighted with so much allegorical machinery that, even after a book and a half, the principal action had not yet begun. Nathaniel recognized the fault and admitted—this a little proudly—that he had followed Milton very closely. The debate of the fallen angels in the court of Pandemonium and the flight of Mammon through Chaos, which later episode filled all of the fourteen pages of Book II, were admittedly imitative. Even the language, he said, "is an attempt to imitate Milton," but used with the best of intentions and with even some idea of improvement on the original:

I have endeavored to communicate to it and to the characters the goodness and grandeur of my immortal example yet I have sometimes ventured to give up the sublime for the natural which in my opinion makes an agreeable variety and by affording the mind some relaxation prepares it to be more forcibly affected by the next bold passage. Though I have conveyed an allegory under the characters, I have made them very little different from those in Milton, except here and there to mark them (as I thought) more strongly. It was my meaning and intention to make my devils like Milton's but I want to know whether the copy bears any resemblance to the original.

Whether at this stage of composition Nathaniel himself had any more than the most nebulous notion of the direction of his epic would take or even of its contents beyond the portion he had written, we have every reason to doubt. "As it would be impossible," he temporized, "for me to give you any idea of the plan and conduct of the poem and of the incidents it is to take in, without writing a volume, I can't now attempt it." But now that the subject, even in vaguest outline, was with him, he wished he might get on with it quickly. "If I was an independent man, I should take great delight in finishing it, notwithstanding its difficulties." But his profession and the necessity of making a living continued in his way. So he proceeded with diffidence because he had "so little confidence in myself and so little hope that the world's taste will agree with mine." If peace had been brought about, as had recently been expected, he might then have dropped everything else and gone on with the epic.

In fact, plans for managing financial matters concerned with *America Delivered* were already worked out—at least to his own satisfaction. He would solicit or, rather, would have his friends in America solicit subscriptions for the work. It would be published in two volumes, six of the proposed twelve books in each volume. He would collect one guinea from each subscriber in advance; then he would collect a second guinea at the time the first volume was published. He estimated that "if five thousand subscribers could have been got in America, the interest on that money would have kept me above want and enabled me to proceed without interruption." He earnestly did want to get it done, "but I had nobody to communicate my plan to and no confidence in the success of its execution and I felt the utter improbability of forming any judgment of a work of which I myself was the author."

The subject seemed so worth while, was filled with such fine poetic promise: "If I could communicate to others that which I felt myself, there would be no doubt of pleasing them." But it was immense, even in contemplation, perhaps too large for him to work within the limits of even an epic frame. "There lies the difficulty in all kinds of writing." When, however, he finally decided to abandon the project, he was persuaded, he insisted, by "another no less powerful reason":

Soliciting a subscription was pledging myself for the execution of a work which I could not foresee whether it would be in my power to execute in such a manner as to merit publication when finished. It was attended with a force and constraint that confined my imagination and made me look forward to its completion like a school boy to end his lesson. It hurried me and prevented me from waiting for those very uncertain returns of enthusiasms which are the wings of the imagination and the Soul of language without which the most laborious efforts of the judgment can bring forth nothing but what is miserable and insipid.

"Enthusiasms which are the wings of the imagination!" Nathaniel was a poet, indeed, and in the most poetical of traditions, catching the elusive inspiration as it fluttered by him, mounting with it to rhapsody or allowing it to plummet him to despair. "Don't suspect me of the affectation of being like Milton when I assure you that these returns of poetic ardour are with me so entirely uncertain that when I begin a thing it is out of my power to guess when it ever shall be finished."

In spite of Sister Bet's criticism, Nathaniel saw much merit in his epic attempt. Readers, his sister told him, would not easily reconcile themselves to the interference by allegorized supernatural forces in events which had taken place before their own eyes. The American Revolution was too real and too recent to be cloaked effectively in the make-believe of poetic tradition. Readers would resent the seeming misrepresentation of incidents which they knew so well at first hand. Nathaniel agreed, with reservations: that, he said, "is the objection to the reading but not to the writing of it at the present time." His eye was on posterity. "Its being written by one who was contemporary with the revolution would in my opinion be an advantage to it when the performance came to be made venerable by the rust of time." Was not that true of other great epics? "The noblest productions of human genius are often not worth a farthing the day they are finished. That was the case with Paradise Lost."

Nathaniel was again not easily discouraged. He was willing to give up his plan of writing an epic, but not because the subject was in any manner unworthy: "I think I could manage it to be firm and poetical." He explained carefully that "the greatest argument against proceeding in it to a man of my indigent circumstances, is the probability of want of encouragement . . . so that though I should like (if I was a man of independence and leisure) to finish it sometime in the course of my life and trust to remote posterity for its fame. I lay it by for the present."

Therefore, he put *America Delivered* aside, and for three reasons. In the first place, "the task was arduous and would have taken up the whole of my time for many years." In the second place, it "could not have been proceeded in without a large subscription," which he had no present means of obtaining. And finally, "upon a late revisal of what I did in it, I perceive I had fallen into too close an imitation of Milton, and I believe if I were to undertake the thing again I should execute it in a different way."

So much for the epic and why Nathaniel did not finish it. But the subject of the Revolution itself was not so readily put aside. If he could not effectively celebrate it in an epic, he would devise some other form better fitted to his talents and his time. "The interest my heart has taken in the American Revolution," he said, "is such as has made me wish not to leave this world without leaving some monument of my sympathy in that truly glorious event in which the obscurity and insignificance of my fortune denied me the happiness of being an actor." Someone would some day recognize its sublime grandeur and write its epic:

As to the Revolution itself, in which the greatest nations of the now populous earth were engaged both by sea and land, in which one of the noblest privileges of human nature was agitated and contended for with the greatest heroism on one side and the greatest obstinacy and perseverance on the other, in which navies encountered such as the ocean never groaned under before, and armies became vanquished and victorious by the effusion of a deluge of blood: this, I say, I can not but think a more bold and sublime subject and scene for the interference of the turbulent spirits of the dark abyss and their hierarchal Antagonists than the capricious determination of our first mother to rob the orchard of Paradise.

Which, in plainer English means, we suppose, that Nathaniel was sure he had a better subject than Milton had.

During the late summer of 1783 he therefore turned his attention to the composition of "a play or rather a mask, the characters allegorical, representing the origin, progress and termination of the war." He described it to St. George as a "mask or opera" and explained that "as America is represented collectively under the

name of Columbinus, I have given that as the title of the performance." The allegorical pattern was suggested by John Dryden's
Albion and Albanius, though "I hope in point of composition,"
Nathaniel primly suggested, it is "superior to the mediocrity of
that work." The manner was unashamedly Shakesperean, and
"judicious friends" in England acknowledged it, said its author, "by
far the best thing I ever wrote": they have "made me vain by
declaring I had not failed much in attempting the style and spirit
of Shakespeare." Lest he sound bumptious, even to his family,
Nathaniel provided a more modest declaimer: "Don't think I am
fool enough to set up for more than an imitator; far be it from
me to pretend to be a rival to that inimitable genius."

New America needed a literature if she were to survive according to the ideals of those who had founded her. A year later, in
the summer of 1784, when peace was secure and the young trans-
atlantic nation faced new problems of independence, Nathaniel explained the necessity to St. George, who may have seemed to him
too deep in American events to view them properly in perspective:

How much it is to the interest of a people to give encouragement
and protection to those who would hold up to the world a picture
of their most noble and exemplary exertions, and build up a monument worthy the admiration of after times, and capable of diffusing
and perpetuating the love of public virtue, I leave to them to determine. Engaged in more sordid pursuits it has been the crime of
nations to neglect their own interest in that of literature, and
suffer those men to languish in indigence whose labors might be
productive of much benefit to the community. How much have
the plays of Shakespeare contributed to diffuse a general knowledge
of some parts of the English history and excited the emulation of
all orders of men in imitating those acts of heroism which they
have seen presented in them. If his noble delineation of the character and fortune of Brutus had been more frequently placed before
their eyes, who knows what effect it might have had in preventing
the savage war we have lately seen terminated?

America did need a literature if she were to become great. And
Nathaniel offered to supply the cornerstone on which it might be
erected.

"Actuated by sentiments of this nature," he had begun the composition of the dramatic *Columbinus* as testimony that his own
devotion to the cause of American liberty was full-hearted and
sincere:

The agitation, anxieties, emotions of indignation and triumph and

sorrow which I have felt as occasion presented through the course of
the war I shall not undertake to describe, but leave you to judge of
them by your own feeling. Let it suffice to say that it was the
subject of all times uppermost in my mind and I return thanks to
Providence that the outcome has been answerable to my prayers
and wishes. Depressed by sickness and discouraged by various
calamities I have nevertheless cherished the love of liberty in a
bosom condemned to be chained to the Lake of Indigence. By day
and by night it has been my favorite theme.

Now, "furnished, like Robinson Crusoe, on an unfrequented coast,
with excellent materials but miserable tools," he constructed in
Columbinus the bark in which, he now was sure, he really would
"voyage over the ocean of time to the distant shore of posterity."

Columbinus has come down to us complete, in a beautifully
written manuscript which, Nathaniel complained, it had taken him
three weeks simply to copy. It is an extended allegory of a type
familiar and popular with readers of his time, like, as Nathaniel
already has said, Dryden's *Albion and Albanius*, like, also, Arbuth-
not's *History of John Bull*, or the American Francis Hopkinson's
A Pretty Story or Jeremy Belknap's *The Foresters*, or *The Divert-
ing History of John Bull and Brother Jonathan* which James Kirk
Paulding wrote many years later. In order to simplify what he
called the "emblematical meaning of the characters," Nathaniel
supplied a postscript for the "use of those readers who do not
choose to be at the pains of unravelling the allegory themselves."
Thus, the character "Albion," he explained, represents the British
nation collectively. "Themis," his wife, stands for "the attribute
of Justice in general but is frequently introduced as the representative of the democratical or popular party in Britain." Albion's
son is "Columbinus," the hero, who is, of course, symbolic of
America. Themis's daughter is "Eleutheria" and she, "as the name
implies can be no other than Liberty for which America contended."
Supporting Columbinus is "Alleghenny," a faithful servant, who
stands for "the two great Agents whose resources were so important
to America, to wit the Congress and the Army, whereof the latter
as a body, may be supposed to have been actuated and directed by
the spirit of the former." With him are "Fidellan," faithfulness or
trust, and "Mingo," a black boy, devoted to his kindly colonial
master. Opposed to Columbinus are "Regan," a courtier, ambitious
and scheming, Albion's representative in America (the Royal colonial government), and "'Bullion," a Caliban-like slave with power

to assume fiendish guises at will, who represents "in general inordinate Wealth, but in particular the overgrown influence of the
crown of Britain, regarded by her constitution as a dangerous Monster." The latter and the greedy power he represents supply much
of the motivation of the action, for to Nathaniel, wealth and the
greed for wealth were at the root of all present evil:

And though princes, viewing it with partial eyes, may hold it an
ornament of the court and a proper attendant of the regal state, it
may in time appear, as it is here represented, pernicious and fiend-
like in its operation. This, at least cannot be denied, that it wears
different shapes in different eyes.

Bullion has two daughters, each of whom assists him in his
evil designs. "Balliadera," product of the rape of a beautiful Per-
sian maiden, is an enchantress, lovely to look upon but evil, and
described in the most lush and oriental phrases Nathaniel could
marshal. She is "Luxury or dissolute pleasure . . . not uncommonly
the offspring of Bullion, or wealth": "How far Luxury and the
spirit of expence, for its own support, may have led to the resource
of taxing America," said Nathaniel, "is left for the reader to judge."
"Gondola," the second daughter, the misbegotten child of an un-
willing Ethiopian mother (herself a symbol of slavery), is a sorcer-
ess representing "the favorers of monarchial and arbitrary power,
the offspring of Bullion, or crown influence." Other characters, less
essential to the plot, but necessary for rounded allegory, are
"Darmstadt," the German, and "Gaul," "Iberian," and "Belgias,"
each representing with less verbal disguise a country which watches
or takes part in the conflict.

Greatly simplified, the bare allegorical argument is as follows:
Britain (Albion), led on by Wealth (Bullion), has an affair with
Luxury (Balliadera), at which his wife, Justice (Themis), leaves
him. Treacherous Regan (his governor in America) convinces
Albion that Liberty (Eleutheria) is plotting against him, leading
his son, Columbinus, also to revolt. Albion's forces battle Columbinus, until Justice returns with France at her side to turn the tide
of battle. As the curtain falls, Columbinus is joined to Eleutheria,
the forces of evil having all been routed, and Albion bows in con-
trite humility to America and to France.

But Nathaniel wove, and with some occasional skill, a tapestry
of song and declamation and of intricate development of the
allegory until *Columbinus* became under his enthusiastic hand "as

long as the longest of Shakespeare's." When the scene opens on the American coast, Albion and Themis appear "seated in a triumphal car drawn by sea-horses; Columbinus, Eleutheria, Tritons and Nereids attending." A chorus of the latter break into welcoming song:

> Let shouts of triumph shake the maine
> to mighty Albion's and to Themis' reign!
>
> Victor from the wat'ry plain
> lo! Albion comes with all his train,
> proud monarch of the foaming tide,
> royal Themis by his side:
> over land and over sea
> clarion sound of jubilee,
> and shouts of triumph ring again
> to mighty Albion and to Themis' reign!

A long first act, unrelieved by action, introduces the principal characters, outlines the ideas which will motivate the development of the plot, and points out the conflict within Albion on which the drama turns. Now, married to Themis, he is both powerful and just. When Regan, his counselor, brings gifts which loyal subjects have sent as token of their love and fealty, the king agrees with his consort that it ill becomes a monarch "with rapacious hand" to despoil his subjects by force,

> to drain the cup
> of patient labour, or like blood-suckers
> to drink up and consume the vital treasure
> that nourishes men's hearts.

He would accept only what was rightly due. If too much were given, let them, he tells his counselor, the overplus be returned:

> O, if kings knew
> to turn the generous current of men's wills
> to good account, not choke up with disdain
> and dry the springs of loyalty when most
> they wish to exceed, how wou'd the prosperous stream
> flow plentiful to drench the thirsty bowels
> of feverish pomp herself, and enough left
> the tender grass to feed and natural plants
> i' the garden of god's earth!

But there was another side to Albion, older than his marriage to Justice, and revealed in his attitude toward the hideous monster-slave Bullion who gathers treasures from all over the world for the

king, his master.   Like Shakespeare's Caliban in *The Tempest,*
whom he in so many respects resembles, Bullion has some of the
most effective lines in this play.   American literature was soon to
become and long to remain so genteel that such words as these
which Nathaniel put in the mouth of his monster must have been
something of a shock even to his worldly brother in Virginia:

> An he do eat us
> We'll stir up such a turmoil in his guts
> As never colic gendered there.

"Miscreated savage," roars Albion, "where's the gold I sent thee
to collect?"   And the monster, fawning, replies:

> 'tis all piled up and counted.   I have ransack'd
> the greedy ocean's maw for conceal'd treasures;
> search'd all the cavernous deeps, and out o' the
> skulls of fishes cull'd the unown'd gems there hid;
> from the slug oyster, shrin'd in mother of pearl,
> pluck'd his round precious trap; wedges of gold
> weigh'd from the sandy bottom; roam'd the shores
> and rocks at ebb-tide after storms for wrecks
> cast thitherward; from the hot bark of trees
> that weep rich gums, gather'd the costly tears;
> swept beds of rivers; rich Pactolus' sands
> sifted; torn up the ponderous ribs of earth
> in fire to torture them, and from smelted ores
> pour'd off the purer metal. . . .

The greed thus fed by fiendish means is to be Albion's downfall.
When he and his queen, with Columbinus and Eleutheria, who
have talked of nobler things through many pages, leave the stage,
then scheming Regan and evil Bullion plot the downfall of the
king's better advisors and their own ascendancy to control over his
royal purse and power.   To reach this end they plan to lure him
deep into the forest, where Bullion's treasure-store is hidden, and
there confront him with the irresistible Balliadera.

In the second act Albion's downfall is effected against a back-
ground of exotic song and prurient chatter from luscious attendant
nymphs as the king is led to a sylvan bower by Bullion's beautiful
daughter, the queen and all good intentions forgotten completely:

> On couch of roses
> He reposes;
> Love's soft pillow lends his down
> To be prest on
> Let him rest on
> Free from thorns that line the crown.

When Regan then enters to announce that Eleutheria, who we remember is the spirit of Liberty, has roused subjects against Albion, the deluded king orders her banished. But he is troubled in mind and allows his new lover to lead him to her half sister, the soothsayer Gondola, who, like the witches in *Macbeth*, sings evil incantations:

> Thrice, and thrice, and thrice the ground
> with iron wand I circle round,
> thrice the mutter'd charm I spread
> and utter sounds that wake the dead.
> Fires that glare and fiends that rule,
> arise from the infernal pool!
> arise! arise! arise!

Then the ground opens and flames ascend, in which Gondola reads to Albion this portent concerning Eleutheria:

> If she wed with Columbine
> this kingdom is no longer thine.

Now we are in the midst of the action, as the third act opens with another weird and Shakespeare-like scene at Bullion's forge, where the fiend is manufacturing a chain to bind Columbinus, until he is discovered by Themis, who steals the chain and departs, she says, for France. Then Columbinus and Eleutheria approach the king in his palace, the young man to plead that the girl be reinstated to her former place of high esteem. Albion, still enthralled by luxury and desire for wealth, orders his guards to seize her, but Columbinus intervenes to allow her escape. Bullion and his hideous daughter set out in pursuit but soon return, Gondola bruised and mangled by Alleghenny, who has rescued the distressed Eleutheria. When Columbinus departs, he meets his sturdy henchman in the forest, who tells him of having come upon Eleutheria, bound to a tree, naked to the waist, while Gondola, the evil child of Bullion, scourged her. Alleghenny presents Columbinus with the bloody cloth with which he had bathed Eleutheria's lacerated back— a cloth of thirteen crimson stripes which Columbinus straightway vows shall be the banner which will lead him to victory.

The king's noble son addresses his followers as they prepare in the fourth act for battle: "Friends, warriours, countrymen," what is it for which we fight? It is

> for liberty; that is, the common benefits
> of light and air; the privilege to breathe

and walk upon God's earth, his free-born creatures,
gathering the blessings his bounty hath plac'd in reach,
with use and exercise of our opinions
to guide our steps: not push'd on by hard taskmasters
whither they list, against our wholesome wills;
not manacled or fetter'd; not bow'd down
with heavy burdens like the brute beasts, whose patience
argues defect of reason. Sirs, we fight for
the name of human creatures; that distinction
which separates man from beast, brave souls from idiots,
th' ambitious rider from the horse that carries him.

Spurred by such sentiments, Columbinus's forces are at first triumphant; but, later, Albion, joined by German mercenaries, puts them to rout and throws their noble leader into prison.

As Columbinus is being led to the scaffold at the beginning of the last act, in rushes Alleghenny and all his men to rescue him and drive the German scoundrels who guard him from the field. This is no sooner done than Themis enters with Gaul, whose armies have arrived just in time to turn the tide of battle at Yorktown. The king, vanquished and repentant, is united again to Themis; Alleghenny enters with the severed head of Regan, "whose hot breath first blew up the coals of war"; and Columbinus joins hands with Eleutheria seated triumphant on her gorgeous throne. The curtain falls as the beautiful, and now reformed, Balliadera sings a new song which Themis has taught her:

> O world, lift up your eyes!
> War's heavy clouds are drift away,
> And in serener skies,
> Bright as the clear star that foreruns the day,
> A new constellation, see
> As the storm dies,
> Begins to rise
> Out of the bosom of the troubled Sea!
> It is the star of Liberty,
> Daughter of the giant War,
> From his dead ashes sprung to blaze afar
> The phoenix of the skies!
> Her light, America, she bends on thee
> And greats the nations all that glory to be free!

As we have skipped thus quickly through the 120 closely written pages of *Columbinus*, taking advantage of shortcuts to avoid the intricacies with which Nathaniel both complicated and explained details of plot and allegory, we find the play, for all its occasional

boisterousness, lacking the sustained, swiftly moving action necessary
to success in presentation. Instead of progressing straightforwardly,
it moves back upon itself more than once, as it painstakingly under-
lines what Nathaniel called the "emblematical meanings." Almost
every incident of dramatic significance takes place off stage, to be
recited afterwards in detail by characters who posture through long
speeches compounded of shreds and patches of worn Shakespearean
fustian. The settings alone, ranging from the bosom of the ocean
to the bowels of the earth, with forest and palace and hilltop used
each in turn, present practical difficulties in stagecraft which, even
in our better mechanized days, would be difficult of solution. The
business of flames leaping from bare boards at the wave of Gondola's
wand, of Bullion rising from the waters of the ocean, or of Eleutheria suddenly materializing for the finale seated in splendor
on an elevated throne, though none of them impossible on the
eighteenth-century stage, are each perhaps better suited to the magic
of modern Hollywood.

But so successful did *Columbinus* seem to Nathaniel, and so
heady was the praise confided to him by the discriminating few to
whom he showed it, that during the summer of 1783 he set himself
to the composition of a second drama, this time a more conventional five-act tragedy, designed especially "for the English stage."
"I have just now finished," he wrote Sister Bet in July, "but not begun to copy." The new play was to be called *The Queen of Jewry*,
and its subject was the death of Mariamne as recorded by the historian Flavius Josephus in Book One of his *The War of the Jews*.
Nathaniel intended to submit to managers of both London theaters,
"though," he admitted, "with small hopes of success" and with little
chance of realizing much from it. "I am sorry to tell you that if
I succeed in bringing in the Queen of Jewry, the pecuniary benefits
to myself will be far less than you would imagine. The author,
it seems now a days is only indulged with three nights benefit,
which, even in case of a full house, will not bring him more than
two or three hundred pounds." But even this, though a small sum,
Nathaniel admitted "would be of service to me at present."

This time his play was better articulated and kept within the
limits of conventional dramatic presentation. The plot was little
altered from the old story recorded by Josephus. King Herod departs from Jerusalem for an interview with Caesar (in Josephus,
it is Anthony), confiding his wife, whom he loved beyond all things,

to the care of Joseph, his sister Salome's husband, with private instructions that if he did not return, Mariamne should also be put to death so that she should never belong to another man. Joseph, anxious to convince the queen of the strength of the king's affection, tells her of the command. When her husband returns safely, Mariamne informs him that she knows his injunction to Joseph; whereupon Herod becomes frantic with jealousy, for he is sure the secret could only have been disclosed by Joseph to the queen in a moment of intimacy; and, his rage fed by insinuations from Salome, he orders Mariamne's instant death. Nathaniel's principal departure from his source was to portray the queen, not as history remembers her, a bitter and revengeful woman who despised her brutal husband, but as a loving and loyal wife whose innocent death results from the tragic flaw of jealousy in Herod's noble nature.

Again Shakespeare was the model for Nathaniel's dramatic method and for the rhythm, even sometimes the imagery of his lines. But even with Josephus to support him on one side and Shakespeare on the other, Nathaniel stumbled more than once. He was best in the angry, ranting lines through which Herod condemned Mariamne, or in the tender lines in which she told her love for him; he was poorest in shaping scenes and incidents for which history gave him no precedent, or in portraying depth or subtlety of character. The verse was competent and mediocre, never rising even to the small heights of enthusiastic rhetoric which Nathaniel had sometimes formerly attained. Most of its was humorless, passionless, tired verse. If we did not remember that Nathaniel was still in his very early thirties, we might say it was tired and middle-aged verse; but if it was, Nathaniel certainly did not recognize it now as such. However inexpert or imitative, *The Queen of Jewry* was his present pride, and he copied it carefully to send to his brothers in America.

Nathaniel felt very strongly that if the tragedy were to be presented in London, then the unashamedly pro-American *Columbinus* would have to be suppressed, at least for the present, "which," he explained, "I did not at first intend to do, for it was my intent to offer it for presentation on the American Stage." But a reputation in England for having written so fervent a celebration of England's defeat was manifestly to be avoided, particularly by a young man who was to look to Englishmen for the advancement of his career, most particularly to a young man with his eye on success on the London stage: "It would damn my last play if it were to get around."

Nathaniel was therefore "induced to let . . . necessities get the better of . . . inclination and conceal for the present" any hint of his authorship of *Columbinus.* "The ardent inclination I have to get possession of the English stage and distinguish myself by a series of dramatic exhibitions, has induced me to suppress the publication of Columbinus . . . because it would doubtless make me unpopular here and might give an opportunity to illnatured persons that chose, to form a party and damn any play that I might hereafter bring forward."

Such sly precautions, however, were not quite necessary, for neither the manager of Covent Garden nor the manager of Drury Lane was interested in producing *The Queen of Jewry.* "Natty is a little in the dumps," wrote Colonel Tucker. "'A play of his, which I understand, had great merit, has been lately refused by the managers of both playhouses." Brother Henry in Bermuda passed the news on to St. George: "These things you know require interest so that the reception of a manager is no argument at all that a piece is devoid of merit." Nathaniel wrote more cheerfully. "I am not absolutely discouraged," he said, "from engaging once more in a similar enterprise."

He was still restless and unsettled. In the spring of 1784 Colonel Tucker wrote once more that "Natty was well and getting into practice, though," he now added, "I am afraid rather slowly, and he has talked much of late of coming out again to America." Perhaps it was this latter plan, which had apparently never completely left him, of settling somewhere nearer to his brothers which led him to write to St. George again—after what seems to have been several years of silence. Sometime, when he had more leisure, he would bring his brother up to date on the adventures and misfortunes which had filled his days since they had parted almost ten years before. Meanwhile, he sent St. George a copy of *Columbinus* to see whether his brother might not help him launch the literary bark which he still felt sure would carry him and his reputation "to the distant shore of posterity."

The few friends whom Nathaniel had dared allow to read *Columbinus* had, we remember, pronounced it good. They were "confidential friends," said the young poet, "'whose opinion of it is flattering to me." Even Colonel Tucker, not easily impressed by poetry, even his son's, thought it had merit. The manuscript was, therefore, entrusted to him for delivery to St. George. "He will tell you," Nathaniel wrote, "that it is my desire that you should submit it to the perusal of some few of your confidential friends." Then, "if it should be their opinion and yours that it merits to be given to the world, I have no objection to its publication. . . . Neither have I any objection to its being represented on the stage." He would not, however, in either case, want his name to appear. At least for the present it would be safer not to tempt unscrupulous reprisals against whatever literary career he might manage in the future. But he did want the work published. Not only was it his best, but it might make money: "If you can print by subscription in such a form as to produce some emolument to its author, my present situation renders it desireable."

Years passed, and nothing, so far as can be discovered, was heard from Virginia of the publication of *Columbinus*. St. George preserved it carefully and undoubtedly showed it to many of his patriot friends, though the voluminus file of his letters written at this time makes no mention of it. If it had been printed then, just at the close of the American Revolution, *Columbinus* would have been the first of the new nation's long patriotic poems. It would have antedated Joel Barlow's fervent *The Vision of Columbus* by two years, and might have appeared even before Timothy Dwight's *The Conquest of Canaan*, which most readers recognized as implicitly patriotic. Like Philip Freneau and John Trumbull and other young men whose careers were distorted by the war in America, Nathaniel sang the new spirit in old words. It seems fitting, then, to enroll his name on the same scroll with theirs and, through recognition of his small achievement in *Columbinus*, to provide him, also, with a more solid paragraph in the history of American literature.

But, as time passed and nothing was heard from America of *Columbinus*, Nathaniel changed to the point that he was at length willing to put poetry and every worldly ambition behind him. Even two years later he could dismiss his patriotic drama by casually suggesting that "if that work should ever have the effect in promoting public virtue, which I intended in writing it, I shall be amply repaid for the trouble it cost me in composition." He became strangely uninterested in literary fame or even financial benefits derived from literature, and he offered his poem now as his gift to the American people: "I should have recommended to your great men to have it represented annually with great form on some public occasion, such as a meeting of Congress, or at the time of some public ceremony, that the memory and understanding of so important a revolution, and the patriot spirit which gave birth to it, might be kept alive and perpetuated."

As for himself, he turned happily to other things. *Columbinus* celebrated "probably the last event in the political world I shall ever feel my heart so interested in, as to write upon." The rest of his life was to be devoted "to a subject which I think of infinitely more importance to mankind."

PEACE

This . . . I have learnt, that I am rich enough if I can be contented with what I have, and with that situation in which Providence most wise has placed me, and this degree of contentment I find no great difficulty in preserving, under the full conviction which I entertain that all things are disposed for us to the promotion of our best interest and happiness, if we will only be content, and endeavour to do our duty in the situation we are placed in.

NATHANIEL TUCKER TO ST. GEORGE TUCKER, 1790

EARLY IN 1786 Nathaniel moved from Malton to the flourishing seaport town of Hull, where, he informed his relatives in Bermuda, he was "better satisfied with prospects" and might establish himself more solidly in the practice of medicine. His letters were humble now and chastened, as he entered again regularly into correspondence with his brothers. He was thirty-six, and tired. He spoke less often of success, and seemed to settle quietly into living, satisfied with the routine of professional duties, his longing for literary distinction apparently subdued completely. He hoped St. George would write him often—"whenever you think I deserve to be forgiven for my silence."

Not until several years later did he admit the cause of what he then described as his "waning hope." It was "in consequence," he explained in 1790, "of an attachment to a young lady in this neighborhood with whom I was under engagements of marriage, but those engagements at her desire were dissolved five or six years ago." And the engagement was "not likely ever to be renewed; she is since moved from hence to Leeds." By this time, so many years later, he could even be dispassionate in retrospect, finding cause, he wrote St. George, to be thankful that the affair had worked out as it had:

You know what it is to experience an *involuntary* separation from one we love, but perhaps not what it is to experience a *voluntary* and unexpected one in a case where discussion seemed an impossibility, and where affection and confidence in one part were without bounds. Yet it is the power of the Divine Providence in the government of contingencies, that even seeming impossibilities are affected. I acknowledge its operation in the present instance with the profoundest gratitude.

This did not sound like the Nathaniel whom St. George had known some ten years earlier—in spite of all his former flights of fancy and conventionally high-flown rhetoric. "What I have reason greatly to be thankful for," he went on, "is, that I seem to be delivered from several passions, which formerly made my life uneasy and restless." He was happy to be harried no longer with "inordinate love of pre-eminence, and thirst after fame, and ambitious distinctions, which never were or could be gratified and consequently never left me at ease." He saw now "the madness and unhappiness" of ambition: "I can never enough be thankful for being disengaged from such enemies to repose."

His brothers were sincerely disturbed by this seemingly sudden transformation. Thomas Tudor wished he and St. George might have a "long conversation on the subject of Natty," who seemed to him "under fanaticism." "Poor Natty," wrote brother Henry from Bermuda. He certainly did not sound like himself at all when he admitted that though "truly my stock of worldly wealth is but small and has hitherto not been adequate to my necessities, yet I can say with truth that my material happiness is infinitely greater than ever it was."

He seemed to be living now, if his letters can be believed, just such a life as he had celebrated in *The Anchoret*, without bitterness, but with a strange, new, and—to his brothers—alarming contentment. "I live in lodgings," he explained, "where my food is provided and brought up to me by a man servant, the only one I keep. I have no horse as I found it attended with an inconvenient expence, but hire one or go in a chair when I am wanted." His practice was not large, but "brings me in generally about £200 a year, a sum sufficient for me to subsist upon according to the frugality and retirement in which I live." It was "carried on without much fatigue in general, a circumstance," said Nathaniel, "very happy for me, as I have not force of constitution to bear me through great difficulties, though," he hastened to add, "my health situated as I am, is commonly good."

He neither expected nor desired ever to rise higher in his profession, "for I have learnt that I am rich enough if I can be contented with what I have," satisfied to allow a divine Providence far wiser than he to provide his share of happiness: "For the last three or four years I don't find that my business has increased, nor do I think that from my turn of mind, character and mode of life that it is likely so to do, for as I have not more skill than my brethren, and at the same time do not wish to give away to any too great eagerness in gathering riches, it is not likely that emoluments will come without being sought after." He was content thereafter, he said, to do his daily duty to the best of his admittedly limited abilities.

This, thought his brothers, was indeed carrying literature too far. But it was not from literature or reaching for poetry that Nathaniel discovered his new-found satisfaction. At thirty-seven, after fifteen years of struggling, fifteen years which found his literary aspirations, it seemed, thrust down each time he bravely raised them, which found him little better established than he had been when he started, after disappointment in ambition and in love, Nathaniel was ready for retreat into himself, weakened perhaps to the point at which retreat was necessary. Living when he did, developing as he had developed, nothing was more natural than that he should find a true, new faith, more important for himself and all mankind, he said, than ever poetry was, and more important even than the "political and consequently temporal situation" of man.

His personal search for happiness had been long, and, because of himself and the troubled times through which he moved, had led to no satisfactory end. Poetry, which had once beckoned him on so bewitchingly, now seemed an incompetent, even a misleading guide. Success was—well, success, like fame, simply had not come to Nathaniel. Even the familiar religion of his fathers, never a burdensome thing, but once comforting in assurance that its adherents were superior to other men and were required, therefore, to lead and to command—even this traditional Anglican faith proved inadequate. It seemed now to be veiled in "impenetrable obscurity" and revealed in "forms monstrous," with none of the simpler "beauty, symmetry, and proportion" which he had with new humility discovered in the revelations of Emanuel Swedenborg, of "whose divine mission and authority," said Nathaniel, "I entertain not the least doubt."

And so Nathaniel, tired perhaps, found in Swedenborg an appropriate fresh enthusiasm, a satisfying enthusiasm for quietness and for submission which freed him from any obligation to pride or arrogance or what his family called success. He became a servant then, and devoted to anonymous good deeds, continuing to write but careful that his name never appeared again during his lifetime on a title page. The aspiration revealed in his early poems, the groping through a stylized and literary humanitarianism toward the core of genuine goodness in Nathaniel which his brothers misread when they pitied him, must almost have seemed prostitution now. To yearn in verse for simplicity in retirement, then to place that verse on auction in exchange for fame, did not, to the new Nathaniel, seem rational at all.

Public espousal of Swedenborg or his teachings was in 1787 neither quite respectable nor, if one valued his reputation, quite wise. But this was no deterrent to Nathaniel. He spent all the money he could spare in purchasing the theologian's works, and all the time he could spare laboriously turning the most useful of them from Latin into English. "You will be surprised," he told St. George, "when I tell you that I devote much of my time to study"— and to study "in which you may possibly think that little clear and satisfactory information is to be obtained." It was a secret activity, and he enjoined silence from his brother when he sent him a package of Swedenborg's works: "Do not give any intimation of the nature of the books to the captain who bears them, because I do not desire my opinions in this respect to be known as yet, for this reason that I believe almost the whole world would consider me as a mad man."

Nathaniel was again completely carried away with enthusiasm. "Be not surprised when I assure you after much study (for it is difficult)" that Swedenborg's writings contain the "only clue to a knowledge of the source and principles, consequently the nature of all things in the material world even, as well as the spiritual." On the nature of the Trinity and of redemption, for example, it made darkness suddenly visible:

These are rendered so clear and plain to every understanding that nothing can be clearer. The fact is this. The same (or an analogous kind of Trinity) exists in man, and this is clearly explained, but man is at this day (though he was not always) ignorant of it by reason of his perversion whereby he has almost excluded all intellectual knowledge, in which is comprehended the nature of his own soul and mind.

The explanation perhaps needed tighter reasoning than Nathaniel was capable of giving it, but he plunged devoutly ahead:

You will find it was the Deity himself who assumed a human form (for reasons not difficult to comprehend when the constitution of the universe and the nature of his government of it seems to be understood) and lived upon earth under the name of Jesus Christ

and that the sphere of his influence which will be explained after
he had made his humanity divine, is the holy spirit. This is similar
in some sort to a sphere exhaling from man which draws others
into sympathy with him or antipathy. Thus the Divinity consists,
not of three *persons*, but three essentials, soul, body and operation
. . . all united in the person of Jesus Christ, of whose character a
most intimate knowledge may be obtained by an acquaintance with
the *interior* sense of the sacred writings, throughout which the
secrets of his wonderful transactions and government are perpetually
displayed.

These "truly divine" writings "contain even to every jot and
tittle, wisdom which cannot be exhausted by angels themselves to
all eternity." Nathaniel wished he could talk with St. George about
them: "I might explain what I know and have learned on the
subject which would fill you with surprise beyond any thing that
has ever come to your ears." Lacking that opportunity, he recommended the writings to his brother's "attentive and candid perusal,"

not doubting that with your impartial love of truth you will rather
be diligent to search after the true meaning and spirit of his writings with a desire first clearly to understand them, before you allow
your mind to occupy itself in the starting of difficulties and objections in regard to a series of information which to me indeed wears
only the aspect of genuine and self evident truths, and that to such
a degree that I am filled with astonishment at the incredulity and
indifference wherewith they have been received by the world.

He asked his brothers to read with patience, until they, too,
discovered that Swedenborg's precepts were "rendered so clear and
plain to every understanding that nothing can be clearer." But
none of them could make anything at all of the writings which
Nathaniel so surreptitiously sent them, neither of his own explanation nor of Swedenborg himself. Thomas Tudor was bewildered
completely by his brother's extraordinary transformation, about
which he was so mysterious, almost conspiratorial in demanding
secrecy. "What do you make of Natty?" he asked St. George. He
himself simply could not get through the books, but he acknowledged with some masculine condescension that Sister Bet in Bermuda seemed to read them with sympathy and understanding.
Brother Henry was most blunt: "Poor Natty," he said, "seems to
have taken a religious turn—he affects to persuade us of his contentment, but in doing so he speaks (in my opinion) the language
rather of dissatisfaction and disgust." But all of the brothers were
glad that, in spite of the new fanaticism, Nathaniel seemed, by every

report, to prosper "with better prospects than formerly." His nephew, George Bruère, called on him at Hull and "was tenderly received and entertained by him."

Nathaniel evidently found in Swedenborg what many equally good and impressionable men found in Emerson fifty years later, a source of refreshment and solace. He fitted so well the times which began to find the rational precision of the eighteenth century incapable of explaining the irrational conduct of man. The transcendental truths which Swedenborg expounded and which, perhaps as far as any man can, William Blake explained, provided Nathaniel an opportunity to escape with satisfaction from a world of competition for which neither his training nor his temperament fitted him, to a more pleasant world modeled to his own, now tired capabilities. "What adds to my contentment," he explained, "is that I have for the most part sufficient time both for reading and contemplation. . . . What I most regret is, that I am not so useful to others as I could wish to be; but at this I desire not to murmur, being conscious that I am not worthy of such gratification as must arise from having it in one's power to be a great benefactor to mankind."

In 1788 his translation, the first in English, of Swedenborg's *The Wisdom of Angels Concerning Divine Love and Divine Wisdom* was published in Manchester under the auspices of the Society for Printing, Publishing, and Circulating the Writings of Swedenborg. It was a labor of love, for which Nathaniel sought return neither in reputation nor coin, issued anonymously, so that not even his brothers in America seem to have suspected his part in it. It was a good translation, and well received, reprinted four times before it was revised in 1835 by the Rev. T. B. Hayward and again in 1843 by Dr. J. J. G. Wilkinson. Nathaniel worked carefully to render the theologian's meaning as exactly as possible: "Throughout the Whole of this Translation," he said in his Preface, "my Aim hath been to give the Reader as little of my own, and as much of the Author and his meaning as possible." But he was cautious also, and when he came on a passage which seemed too openly pantheistic, he omitted it from his version, "supposing it too strong for the public stomach."

There is no question of Nathaniel's devotion, his complete submerging of his own formerly aspiring personality to what he now considered the higher and more sublimely inspired truths of Emanuel Swedenborg. "This estimable Work," he told his readers, "may be compared to a golden Key, long lost and hid among Rubbish, but now at last found, whereby under the Divine Blessing, a Door may be unlocked, and the Reader introduced to inexhaustible Treasures of true Religion and true Philosophy." Nor was Nathaniel's dedication to his new task simply a thing of the moment. Two years later his second translation, this time *The Wisdom of Angels Concerning the Divine Providence*, was issued by the same Swedenborgian society. Reprinted twice, this also remained the standard English edition for almost half a century, until it was revised in 1833 by Alexander Maxwell.

These books circulated widely, sometimes apparently as a two-volume set. A correspondent to the *New-Jerusalem Magazine* in 1791 reported that "the number of readers is every day increasing, not only in this town [Manchester], and neighborhood, and kingdom, but also throughout Europe." Swedenborgian societies were springing up, sometimes surreptitiously, in England and America. Nathaniel's translations provided the principal texts used for their study of the newly revealed divine mysteries. One admirer, writing in the Manchester *Chronicle*, asserted that no other writings, ancient or modern, contained such "great truths of revelation relating to the creation, redemption, and regeneration of man, opened, explained, and enforced with so much clearness, simplicity, and power." Until he had read Nathaniel's translations, he had been led by popular prejudice to imagine Swedenborg a madman.

Thus, quietly appearing in the service of another man, Nathaniel reached an audience such as he had never reached with his own writings. Even poets who certainly would never have been moved by his poetry read him with interest now. William Blake, for example, owned both the *Divine Love and Divine Wisdom* and the *Divine Providence* in Nathaniel's translation, and he annotated them freely as he prepared his ambitious poetical renderings of the Swedenborgian doctrine. Samuel Taylor Coleridge also scrawled marginal notes in his copy of Nathaniel's first translation. His were the volumes which Wordsworth must have read, and Robert Southey, and many another young man who at the turn of this century was finding in Swedenborg an antidote to the neatly packaged, rational concepts of his elders.

Perhaps, then, it is in these volumes, which fed poets whose verse does live, that Nathaniel inadvertently fashioned the small bark which has unobtrusively carried his literary influence to those distant shores of posterity toward which he had formerly looked with such longing. When he stopped trying, when he no longer worried about success, then he succeeded. He did not attempt now to pour his own unformed aspiration into literary molds provided by other men. He worked painstakingly and lovingly, we suppose, simply to express clearly the inspired truths which Swedenborg revealed. His own aspiration and his certainty of some essential goodness in himself and all men, for which he had never been able to find the proper words, were made plain to him, and through him to men much greater than he, in the writings which he now translated. So Nathaniel becomes, almost in spite of himself and certainly unconsciously, one of the instruments which helped shape the renaissance of wonder which we remember as the Romantic Movement. His brothers, developing to solid respectability in the new and busily successful United States, never understood this.

In the summer of 1791 his third translation from Swedenborg, *The Apocalypse Revealed*, appeared in two volumes and remained the only edition of this work in English for more than forty years. It was his most ambitious undertaking, over twelve hundred closely printed pages, and on a subject even more difficult than he had attempted before. By June of that year he was at work on a fourth translation, apparently at the request of the Swedenborgian society, to provide a version of *A Treatise Concerning Heaven and Hell, and of the Wonderful Things Therein* more correct than that first issued in 1778 by William Cookworthy and Thomas Hartley. It would be done "by the same able hand, and with the same exactness as was employed in the version of the *Divine Wisdom* and *Divine Providence*," promised the official *New-Church Magazine*, "in order that a more faithful and literal translation than the first may appear." This certainly was fame, though in anonymity. Nathaniel was valued and appreciated then by those who knew of his activities as a translator. And he is remembered by modern Swedenborgians as an important and active "early light of the New Church."

It may have been his marriage on September 7, 1791, which interfered with Nathaniel's completion of this, his last literary project. His bride was Jane Wood, second daughter of a tar merchant in Hull, a pious young lady, well born but not wealthy, whose interest in good deeds was as great as his own. Perhaps adjustment to the multitudinous details of married life by a bachelor now over forty made quiet hours in his study no longer possible. Perhaps, as later correspondence with his brothers hints but does not quite prove, his bride was not as enthusiastic about the Swedish theologian as was her husband. She was a woman, said Thomas Tudor, "of extraordinary merit," whose benevolence, however, seems to have found most satisfaction in more practical things, in visiting the poor, in attending religious meetings, and in producing a large family of young Tuckers.

When two years later Frances Bruère Tucker visited her brother in Yorkshire, she found Nathaniel's wife "in the straw with a son called Abel," a dear little fellow but sadly disfigured by a harelip of which the devout physician father took no notice until his sister insisted that he have it operated upon. It was a very great pity, felt Mrs. Tucker, that her brother "had taken such a Methodistical turn, as he would otherwise have had all the practice of Hull which is a very growing opulent sea port town." It also seemed "unfortunate that he has married a woman of equal a grave turn as himself, and as much bigoted to that sect as he is." If Jane Tucker had "been of a lively turn, she might perhaps have roused him a little." As things stood, "they appear to be very fond of each other and don't seem to wish to rise at all with the world."

From this time onward, Tuckers across the Atlantic heard less and less of Nathaniel and his growing family. By 1802 there were five children, four girls and a boy, all delicate and all fated to die young. In 1794 Nathaniel had become one of the physicians attached to the Hull Infirmary, and he spent more and more of his energies in ministering to patients too poor to pay even his modest fees. He supervised the medical education of one of his nephews from Bermuda and wrote in detail of that young man's health and professional aspirations. His letters, more infrequent now, were objectively reportorial, filled with news of his family, the measles, chicken pox, and scarlet fever which kept one or another of the children so often abed, and the coughing sickness which seemed to lie like an ominous curse on them all. He spoke less often of himself, except that he worked hard and managed with great difficulty to meet growing household expenses. There was nothing of complaint in these later letters, nor any spark of the enthusiasm which made the younger Nathaniel, even when ridiculous, attractive. It was apathy perhaps, possibly middle age, but Nathaniel would have called it contentment.

As years went on, however, his practice fell off—"his profession is laborious," wrote Mrs. Tucker, who had taken wifely charge of correspondence with her husband's family, "and the emoluments inadequate." Nathaniel himself tired easily now. It fatigued him completely to write at all, even letters. Patients left him for a younger competitor, "a vain coxcomb with less merit." By the autumn of 1807 his brothers were seriously alarmed of what they heard of the state of his health. "It is evident," wrote Thomas Tucker, who had great difficulty in deciphering the long, rambling, and unpunctuated letters in which his sister-in-law reported their distress, "that the mind of his wife and probably his own is mortified by the unmerited success of his rival." But the older brother was glad also to report to St. George that Nathaniel and his wife had now not only given up the unintelligible Swedenborg, but had even reached the point of considering his doctrine dangerous.

Hardly a month afterwards, on December 3, 1807, Nathaniel died at the age of fifty-seven, "a man whose purity of morals and rectitude of conduct in every department of life," said the Hull *Advertiser* two days later, "will render his memory dear to his surviving relatives and friends." Colleagues from the Infirmary attended his funeral in a body; the *Gentleman's Magazine* in London remembered him very briefly as the author of *The Bermudian* and *The Anchoret*, "both quartos"; his nephew many years later recalled, "I have met with but few persons of more mild, amiable, and dignified demeanor"; but to his brothers, each prosperous now in the United States, he was still "Poor Natty," and they made plans for the provision of his destitute family.

His widow, with her five small children about her, packed hurriedly for departure to a small house in Surrey where she was to live for the next fourteen years. Friends in Hull subscribed for almost seven hundred copies of a new edition of *The Bermudian*, written by their benevolent doctor so many years before, and published again now for the benefit of his bereaved wife. In a hurried, heartbroken letter to St. George in Virginia, Jane Tucker pronounced perhaps her husband's best epitaph: "His life was not one of the highest. . . . He shone best when hid in the bosom of his family. . . . He walked as the fair day without a cloud of concealment from the consciousness of any vice."

BIBLIOGRAPHICAL ESSAY

Unless otherwise indicated, all quoted material, of whatever kind, is from the Tucker-Coleman Collection, on deposit at Colonial Williamsburg, Inc. The correspondence and other manuscripts there assembled are so well arranged, both chronologically and according to writer, that it has seem unnecessary in every instance to identify excerpts with complete details of date, writer, and recipient. Whenever a date or a name is in any way significant to the subject under discussion, I have included it in the text. In other instances I have attempted as discriminating a selection from Nathaniel's correspondence as possible, in order to provide what I hope may be an integrated commentary on his literary career.

CHAPTER I: Best accounts of the early Tuckers are found in Thomas Addis Emmet, *An Account of the Tucker Family of Bermuda from a History of the Emmet Family* (New York, 1898), which contains excellent genealogical information; John William Kaye, *The Life and Correspondence of Henry St. George Tucker, Late Accountant-General of Bengal and Chairman of the East-India Company* (London, 1854); and Mary Haldane Coleman, *St. George Tucker: Citizen of No Mean City* (Richmond, 1938). The Tucker family Bible, in the Virginia Historical Society Library, and the MS "Tucker Genealogical Tree," prepared by Edmund H. Tucker, at Colonial Williamsburg, also supply useful information; as does the letter of October 27, 1813, from St. George Tucker to Richard Rush, printed in Mrs. George P. Coleman, ed., "Randolph and Tucker Letters," *Virginia Historical Magazine*, XLII (1934), 211-22. For Bermuda during this period I have used Philip Freneau, "Account of the Island of Bermuda," *United States Magazine*, I (1779), 31-34, from which the quotation at the head of the chapter is also taken, and Wilfred Brinton Kerr, *Bermuda and the American Revolution* (Princeton, 1936). Verses quoted are, in order, from *The Bermudian* (Williamsburg, 1775), 2; from the MS "Dr. Tucker to Miss Seward in Answer to Her Address to Him on Reading the Bermudian"; and from the MS "To Mrs. Tucker and Miss Tucker" (see "The Writings of Nathaniel Tucker" below). Thomas Tudor Tucker's medical thesis is listed in the *British Museum Catalogue* as *Dissertatio . . . de frigoris in corpus humanum viribus* (Edinburgh, 1770). The complete story of the Tucker brothers remains to be told. Among the papers of the Tucker-Coleman Collection are untapped materials on the career of Henry Tucker, Jr., whose sons were active in colonization of India; on Thomas Tudor Tucker as he retired from medicine to become Treasurer of the United States; and, in especially rich detail, on St. George Tucker as he moved toward wealth and influence in Virginia.

CHAPTER II: For pre-Revolutionary Charleston I have used files of the *South-Carolina Gazette* and the *South-Carolina Gazette and Country Journal*; Alexander Hewatt, *An Historical Account of the Rise and Progress of the Colonies of South Carolina* (London, 1779); Leila Sellers, *Charleston Business on the Eve of the American Revolution* (Chapel Hill, 1934); and, for the quoted material descriptive of the city, the "Journal of Josiah Quincy, Junior, 1773,"

Massachusetts Historical Society Proceedings, XLIX (1916), 424-81. For identification of persons in Williamsburg whom Nathaniel or St. George Tucker mentioned in their letters only by last name or nickname, I have used, in addition to the usual biographical sources, the excellent *A Provisional List of Alumni, Grammar School Students, Members of the Faculty, and Members of the Board of Visitors of the College of William and Mary, from 1693 to 1888* (Richmond, 1941).

The Tucker-Williams controversy is a subject which, even to taking advantage of all materials in Tucker correspondence, I have not treated exhaustively: it may be followed in more detail in the Charleston newspapers mentioned above. Some of Nathaniel's additional remarks on "that Damned scoundrel Williams" are, however, perhaps also worth recording. To justify himself for having said so many harsh things of Williams in his satirical *Paramythia,* "it may not be amiss," said the young poet, "to give you a hint of one or two notorious anecdotes of him. Having a plantation to sell he made an agreement with a purchaser for a particular price and nothing was wanted to confirm it but delivery of the title and payment of the money, but before the matter was entirely settled, a larger sum being offered, he had the obdurance to demand as much of the purchaser, declaring his intention, in case of his refusal, to withhold the titles and close with the proposal of the person who made the last application. But you will not be surprised at such an instance of the want of probity in a man who not even hesitated to defraud a parent. It is pretty well known here that our hero was once requested by his father to attend a vendue and purchase a certain tract of land in his behalf which was to be offered for sale. The land was knocked off to him and before the titles were made out this dutiful son happening to meet an acquaintance was congratulated on the great and very advantageous bargain he had made. This hint was sufficient and he accordingly took care to have his own name inserted in the conveyance instead of his father's. A remarkable instance of filial gratitude! The conditions of the sale were such that a credit was given and the old man attending the treasurer or tax-gatherer soon after to pay the necessary tax for his newly acquired property was informed to his great surprise that this hopeful son has already satisfied the officer on that head. These circumstances with some others that have already come to your knowledge [see pp. 25-28 above] will serve to cast a light on the character of this genius. I shall only add that in matters where he has been empowered to prosecute in behalf of absent creditors as well as in many cases he has proceeded with so much rigor and want of humanity as to render himself detested by the unhappy objects of his enmity."

CHAPTER III: Reviews of *The Bermudian* are found in the *Gentleman's Magazine,* XLIV (1774), 230, 327, and in the *Critical Review,* XXXVIII (1774), 75; for excerpts from other reviews, see the *Virginia Gazette,* November 3, 1774, p. 3. Mrs. Nicholas's verses in praise of *The Bermudian* are found in John Page's MS notebook in the College of William and Mary Library. For John Adams's comment on the poem, see Coleman, ed., "Randolph and Tucker Letters," 222-23.

CHAPTER IV: No official record seems to exist of Nathaniel's having attended classes at the University of Edinburgh, though we suppose from the tenor of his letters that he was at least for one or more short periods in residence; see also the posthumous edition of *The Bermudian* (Hull, 1808), which describes the poem as "written previously to his being a medical student at Edinburgh." His medical degree, however, was from the University of Leyden.

CHAPTER V: All material in this chapter is from the Tucker-Coleman Collection or from other sources made clear in the text.

CHAPTER VI: For Nathaniel's immersion in Swedenborgian doctrine, see, among others, his letter of February 20, 1787, to St. George Tucker; John Calvin Clark, "The First English Translator of 'Divine Providence,' " *New Church Review*, X (1903), 237-42; William White, *Emanuel Swedenborg: His Life and Writings* (London, 1867), II, 202, 567-97; James Hyde, *A Bibliography of the Works of Emannel Swedenborg, Original and Translated* (London, 1906); and the *New-Jerusalem Magazine*, I (1791), 210, 212, 306. So complete was Nathaniel's careful desire for anonymity in this connection that neither his letters nor the fragmentary early records of the New Church reveal, as far as I can determine, anything further of his participation in the movement. For his connection with the Hull Infirmary, see the *Hull and East Riding Portfolio*, February 1, 1887, and the Hull *Advertiser*, December 7, 1807. For his marriage, see the *Gentleman's Magazine*, XLI (1791), 872.

Nathaniel and Jane Tucker had, altogether, seven children: *Abel*, born in the spring of 1793 (Thomas Tudor Tucker to St. George Tucker, March 1, 1793), was still living in 1795 (Henry Tucker, Jr., to St. George Tucker, May 20, 1795), but is not heard of again thereafter; *Ruth*, born in 1794 or 1795 (Henry Tucker, Jr., to St. George Tucker, May 20, 1795), was reported in 1811 on her deathbed (Thomas Tudor Tucker to St. George Tucker, December 9, 1811) and is not heard of thereafter; *James Justus*, the only child who lived to maturity, was probably born in 1796 (Frances Tucker to St. George Tucker, April, 1804: "they have all a very delicate constitution"); *Jane*, born in 1798 and died September 30, 1811 (*Gentleman's Magazine*, LXXXI [1811], 396); *Eleanor*, born in 1800 and died February 22, 1817 (*ibid.*, LXXXVII [1817], 280); *Ann Elizabeth*, born in 1802 and died February 24, 1817 (*ibid.*, 281); and an infant who died of scarlet fever in 1808 (Thomas Tudor Tucker to St. George Tucker, June 27, 1808).

For Nathaniel's death, see the *Hull Advertiser*, December 7, 1807, p. 3; the *Gentleman's Magazine*, LXXVII (1807), 1174; and the Tucker family Bible. After her husband's death, Jane Tucker, the children, and "two old servants" moved to a small house at Poplar Row, No. 8, Newington, Surrey, a borough, she said, where was found the "cheapest market in London"; rent was £25 a year, taxes £10, but the house was in a "genteel neighborhood" (Jane Tucker to St. George Tucker, December 31, 1807). There, "with the assistance of friends, she got on tolerably well in her pecuniary matters, notwithstanding the heavy expenses arising from the sickness of her children" (Thomas Tudor Tucker to St. George Tucker, October 18, 1808). The two brothers in America sent her money regularly; Thomas Tudor, comfortable in Washington now as Treasurer of the United States, offered to remit £250 every six months, and suggested that St. George add £50 or £100 more (Thomas Tudor Tucker to St. George Tucker, June 27, 1808); her "trials," he reported, "were severe": the children worried her—"Ruth has the spitting which alarms me at times yet I flatter myself she will outgrow this weakness" (Jane Tucker to St. George Tucker, September 6, 1808). She asked advice of her brothers-in-law on James's education——he wanted a military career and nephew Henry Tucker, now in Calcutta, had promised to use his influence to have him enrolled as a cadet in the East Indies, but she disapproved of the profession of arms and wanted her son to go to St. Paul's instead (Jane Tucker to St. George Tucker, September 6, 1808; Thomas Tudor Tucker to St. George Tucker, November 1, 1808).

Letters between St. George and Thomas Tudor Tucker during the next several years often mention their "dear sister in England" and discuss remittances which they can or will send her. She had, thought Thomas Tudor, some little income of her own, and nephew Henry supplied a small annuity of £25 (Thomas Tudor Tucker to St. George Tucker, March 22, 1815, and October 10, 1815), but her pecuniary embarrassments continued, until Thomas Tudor wrote of his "ill-fated sister" and remarked piously that "the most virtuous seem to suffer most frequently" (Thomas Tudor Tucker to St. George Tucker, May 26, 1815). Sickness and misfortune, he said, had increased expenses far beyond her means. He hoped that James's education would be soon completed, so that his mother might have some relief (Thomas Tudor Tucker to St. George Tucker, October 10, 1820); the boy was well spoken of by his instructors, and should do well (Thomas Tudor Tucker to St. George Tucker, May 17, 1820). By 1821 Thomas Tudor thought his sister-in-law finally sinking "under the weight of her afflictions"; all her children were dead except James, and he had been so ill recently that she had been drawn to even greater expenses. Fees at the college were more than she had anticipated. St. George and Thomas Tudor continued to send her money; the latter wanted to fix an annuity of £100 on his sister-in-law, but thought that James, who was now trying unsuccessfully for a curacy, should be able to strike out for himself after one more remittance (Thomas Tudor Tucker to St. George Tucker, June 24, 1821). In the autumn of that year James wrote that his mother's mind had broken "under the weight of afflictions"; then, not many weeks later, he announced her death on September 29, 1821 (Thomas Tudor Tucker to St. George Tucker, September 12, 1821, February 15, 1822). Nephew Henry St. George Tucker, then in London, attended the funeral: she "was followed to her grave by all the decent poor of the nighborhood, among whom I could not discern many dry eyes. This circumstance struck me forcibly; for I knew she had not the means of being charitable; and why, then should the poor weep? I have attended funerals of the opulent and great without a tear shed. I can only conclude that benevolence may supply the place of wealth, and touch the chords of the heart when the hand of munificence may fail to leave an impression" (Kaye, *The Life and Correspondence of Henry St. George Tucker*, p. 7).

James Justus Tucker took orders, soon after his mother's death, and was appointed to an English church in Danzig (Thomas Tudor Tucker to St. George Tucker, February 15, 1822). He was unwillingly a clergyman: "I always thought myself ill qualified, but . . . the voice of my parent . . . prevailed"; and he was lonely in his foreign post: "I associate little with the Germans. My natural inclination is for retirement." He inherited his father's liking for bold figures of speech, when he wrote, "In my present situation, I compare myself to a mariner cast upon a rock and saved from destruction while in safety I behold

on all sides the tempestuous billows which have launched the rest into eternity."
Like his father also, he had optimistic faith that his condition would somehow
improve.   When we last hear from him, he wrote cheerfully that a wealthy
gentleman "who wishes to have his son prepared for the University would put
him under my charge here" (James Justus Tucker to St. George Tucker, April
21, 1823).   No further record survives, but family tradition remembers that he
died soon thereafter.

THE WRITINGS OF NATHANIEL TUCKER

I. PRINTED:

"To Eleazer," *South-Carolina Gazette*, July 9, 1772, p. 2.

This satire is found in MS, attributed in a contemporary hand (St. George Tucker's?) to Nathaniel Tucker, in the Tucker-Coleman Collection, Colonial Williamsburg, Inc.

The Bermudian: a poem. By Nathaniel Tucker. London: printed for the author. Sold by T. Cadell in the Strand, and by W. Creech, Edinburgh. MDCCLXXIV.

4to, pp. (1), 16. Title page contains quotations from Horace (two lines) and Waller (four lines). Actually printed in Edinburgh, probably in January or February 1774. Priced 1s. 6d.

The Bermudian. A poem. Williamsburg: printed by Alexander Purdie & John Dixon. M,DCC,LXXIV.

4to, pp. (4), 15. Title page contains quotation (two lines) from Horace only. Printed in May, 1774, with a dedicatory letter addressed "To Henry Tucker, Junior, Esq; of Bermuda," which does not appear in the Edinburgh edition. Priced 2s. 6d.

"Mr. Clackit to his brotherhood," *The Weekly Magazine, or Edinburgh Amusement*, XXIX (September 12, 1775), 369-70.

Identified in a letter, Nathaniel Tucker to St. George Tucker, September, 1775, and by a clipping from the *Weekly Magazine* in the Tucker-Coleman Collection.

"The Optimist," *The Weekly Magazine, or Edinburgh Amusement*, XXX (November 30, 1775), 303-04.

Signed "N⸺T⸺."

The Anchoret: a poem. By the author of the Bermudian. London: printed for and sold by J. Murray, no. 32 Fleet-Street, and W. Creech, Edinburgh. MDCCLXXVI.

4to, pp. 32. Title page contains quotation (two lines) from Horace. Probably printed in Edinburgh.

Tentamen medicum inaugurale de corporis humani, singulis vitae stadiis, mutationibus, quod annuente summo numine, ex auctoritate rectoris magnifici, Friderici Guilielmi Pestel, juris utriusque doctoris et juris publici privati professoris ordinarii, nec non amplissimi Senatus Academici consensu et noblissimae Facultatis Medicae decreto, pro grado doctoratus, summisque in medicina honoribus et privilegiis et legitime consequendis, eruditorum examini subjicit Nathaniel Tucker, Bermudensis. Ad diem xiv. Augusti. MDCCLXXVII. H. L. Q. S. Lugduni Batavorum: Apud Sam. et Joannem Luchtmans. MDCCLXXVII.

8vo, 48 pp.

"To the fair Incognita who sent a gentleman an anonymous copy of verses on Valentine's Day which were not received till some time after." *Morning Post, and Daily Advertiser*, February 25, 1778, p. 4.

MS copy in Nathaniel Tucker's hand in Tucker-Coleman Collection, which contains also the "Copy of verses sent to N. T. on Valentine's day, 1778" (not printed), but not the "Incognita's answer to her Valentine's verses in Tuesday's paper," which appeared in the *Morning Post*, March 2, 1778, p. 4.

"On Happiness. From the Hermit. A tale. By the author of the Bermudian." Printed in an unidentified volume containing a printed journal written by Margaret Lowther [Mrs. John Page] and several printed and MS poems by Margaret Lowther, St. George Tucker, and others. [Richmond (?), ca. 1790.]

The fact that this excerpt was printed as "From the Hermit" by friends in Williamsburg some years after that poem had been printed in Edinburgh as *The Anchoret* perhaps indicates how little was known in America of the publication of that poem.

The wisdom of angels, concerning Divine Love and Divine Wisdom. Translated from the original Latin of the Hon. Emanuel Swedenborg. London: printed and sold by W. Chalklen, Gracechurch street. 1788.

8vo, pp. (2), 4, xxii, 461, (2). Printed at the expense of the Society for Printing, Publishing, and Circulating the Writings of Swedenborg, Manchester. A copy in the library of the British Museum contains autograph notations by William Blake. Reprinted in London, 1788; in Boston, 1794; in London, 1816. A privately owned copy of the 1816 edition contains autograph annotations by Samuel Taylor Coleridge; see London *Morning Light*, III (1880), 338.

The wisdom of angels concerning the Divine Providence. Translated from the Latin of the Hon. Emanuel Swedenborg. Originally published at Amsterdam, anno 1764. London: printed and sold by R. Hindmarsh, printer to His Royal Highness the Prince of Wales, no. 32 Clerkenwell-close, and may be had by giving orders to any of the booksellers in town and country. 1790.

8vo, pp. xl, 600. With a Preface by the Rev. John Clowes, and published by the Society for Printing, Publishing, and Circulating the Writings of Swedenborg, Manchester. A privately owned copy contains annotations by William Blake; see Hyde, *Bibliography of . . . Swedenborg*, p. 439.

The Apocalypse revealed, wherein are disclosed the arcana there foretold, which have hitherto remained concealed. Now translated from the original Latin of Emanuel Swedenborg, published at Amsterdam, 1766. Vol. i. [II]. Manchester: printed by C. Wheeler, 1791. Sold by Messrs. G. G. J. and J. Robinson, Paternoster Row, and R. Hindmarsh, Clerkenwell-close, London; by T. Miller, bookseller, Bristol; and by J. and W. Clarke, Manchester. [1791.]

An edition of 1000 copies printed at the expense of the Society for Printing, Publishing, and Circulating the Writings of Swedenborg, Manchester.

A summary exposition of the internal sense of the books of Genesis and Exodus, and of the Gospel according to Matthew, and of the Revelations; extracted from the *Arcana coelestia* of Baron Swedenborg, from the new translation of the *Gospel* according to Matthew; and from the

Apocalypse revealed. London: printed and sold by J. and E. Hodson, Cross street, Hatton Garden; also by J. and W. Clarke, Manchester, and all other booksellers. 1807.

12mo, pp. 171. Reprinted from John Clowe's translation of *Arcana coelestia* (London, 1783) and from Tucker's translation of *Apocalypse revealed*.

The Bermudian: a poem. By Nathaniel Tucker. Written previously to his being a medical student at Edinburgh. Hull: printed by Joseph Simmons, Rockingham-office, Bowlalley lane: and sold by Mrs. Browne, and Mr. Rodford, Lowgate, 1808.

4to, pp. (8), 16. Title page contains quotation from Horace (two lines) and from Waller (four lines). On p. [i] the following notice appears: "The Subscribers to the Bermudian are respectfully desired by the Widow of the late Doctor Tucker to accept her most grateful acknowledgments, for the kindness and liberality she and her family have experienced from them. 28th July 1808." One hundred and twenty-nine subscribers are listed for 684 copies.

II. MANUSCRIPTS:

A. An uncatalogued folder, in the Tucker-Coleman Collection, containing verses in the hand of Nathaniel, Elizabeth, and St. George Tucker. Those identified as by Nathaniel Tucker are:

1. "To Mrs. Tuckers and Miss Tucker," signed "N.T." and dated "St. Georges 31st March 1771"; 4 pp. Quoted in part on pp. 8, 9 above.

2. "Paramythia. An Epistle to Eugenius," 20 pp.; see pp. 28-29 above.

3. "To Eleazer," 4 pp., signed "Philalethes"; identical except in minor details of capitalization and punctuation with the poem appearing in the *South-Carolina Gazette*; see p. 14 above.

4. "Epistle to ———," 4 pp., in Nathaniel Tucker's hand; see p. 17 above.

5. "On Miss Christy—by N.T.," 1 p.; quoted in full on pp. 17-18 above.

6. "Jeu d'Esprit by N.T."; the first quartrain quote on p. 17 above.

7. "To Belinda in the Country," 16 lines, in Nathaniel Tucker's hand.

8. "To the Same," five six-line stanzas, in Nathaniel Tucker's hand.

9. "An Acrostick," spelling out "Marianne Smith," in Nathaniel Tucker's hand.

10. "To Miranda," five four-line stanzas, in Nathaniel Tucker's hand.

11. "An Acrostick," spelling out "Effie Smith," in Nathaniel Tucker's hand.

12. "A Copy of Verses sent to N. T. on Valentine's day, 1778" and "An Answer to the foregoing, inserted in the Morning Post,

one of the daily papers," in Nathaniel Tucker's hand;
quoted in part on p. 63 above.

B. Folder No. 370, Tucker-Coleman Collection, which contains:

13. "A Pastoral," 4 pp. (unfinished), attributed in another (Elizabeth Tucker's ?) hand to "N.T."

C. Notebook, in Tucker-Coleman Collection, containing:

14. "Miss Seward to Dr. Tucker on reading his poem the Bermudian," 4 pp., and "Dr. Tucker to Miss Seward in answer
to Her address to him on reading the Bermudian," 14 pp.,
both in Nathaniel Tucker's hand; quoted in part on pp.
5, 67-70 above.

D. Notebook, in Tucker-Coleman Collection, containing:

15. "The Bermudian. A Poem by N. T." Copied by Mrs. Frances
Tucker of Bermuda, 14 pp.

E. Notebook, in Tucker-Coleman Collection, containing:

16. "America Delivered. An Heroic Poem in three Parts. Part
1st. The Triumph of Patriotism or the Defeat of Mammon.
In Six Books," book I, 64 pp., book II (unfinished), 14 pp.,
both in Nathaniel Tucker's hand.

F. Notebook, in Tucker-Coleman Collection, containing:

17. "Columbinus. A Mask," 122 pp., in Nathaniel Tucker's hand.

G. Notebook, in Tucker-Coleman Collection, containing:

18. "The Queen of Jewry. A Tragedy," 93 pp., in Nathaniel
Tucker's hand.

H. Notebook, in Tucker-Coleman Collection, containing:

19. "Supplement to the Queen of Jewry, A Dramatick History,"
51 pp., in Nathaniel Tucker's hand; a rewriting of portions
of the play, keyed to no. 18 above.

INDEX

Date Due